For more than fifteen years, Allan
Scottish edition of *The Sunday T*
A former Journalist of the Year in
is the author of *Inside The Wicker Man*, and *Nileism: The Strange Course of The Blue Nile*. He lives in Glasgow.

50 PEOPLE WHO SCREWED UP SCOTLAND

Allan Brown

Constable • London

CONSTABLE

First published in Great Britain by Constable,
an imprint of Constable & Robinson, 2014

This edition published in the UK by Constable, 2015

3 5 7 9 10 8 6 4

Text copyright © Allan Brown, 2014
Illustrations copyright © David Smith, 2014

The moral right of the author has been asserted.

A CIP catalogue record for this book is available from the British Library.

ISBN 978-1-47211-962-9 (paperback)
ISBN: 978-1-47210-339-0 (ebook)

Typeset in Great Britain by SX Composing DTP, Rayleigh, Essex
Printed and bound in Great Britain by CPI Group (UK) Ltd, Croydon, CR0 4YY

Papers used by Constable are from well-managed forests and
other responsible sources

MIX
Paper from
responsible sources
FSC® C104740

Constable
is an imprint of
Little, Brown Book Group
Carmelite House
50 Victoria Embankment
London EC4Y 0DZ

An Hachette UK Company
www.hachette.co.uk

www.littlebrown.co.uk

This book is dedicated to
Leonard Cohen
Siobhan Synnot
and Trembling Bells

'The Celt is supposed to be spiritually superior to the Saxon — simpler, more creative, less vulgar, less snobbish, etc. — but the usual power hunger is there under the surface. One symptom of it is the delusion that Scotland could preserve its independence unaided and owes nothing to British protection.'

George Orwell, 'Notes on Nationalism', 1945

Contents

Acknowledgements

I would like to thank Kenneth Wright for prompting and helping refine so much of what follows, and Kevin Pocklington of Jenny Brown Associates; an Englishman whose relocation north and subsequent determination to see this book published may not have been coincidental. Also, Adrian Gill for the foreword and Edwin Moore who furnished numerous helpful suggestions, few of which I could use on the grounds that Edwin appears to know what he's talking about. Thanks also to Michael Mann, Chris Barnett and Andreas Campomar at Constable, Chris Deerin, Julie, Jim and Scott, my mother and father, Martin Gray, Holly Wright-Gray and Joseph Thomas Brown. Thanks for existing, Trembling Bells, in fondest memory of Sharon McCord Hon FRIAS.

Foreword

The fifty names who follow comprise a brilliant cast of villains. The temptation must have been to take a conventionally historical approach; but, really, who cares what the Earl of Montrose did in 1574? What we have here is a very Scottish way round the problem. Were you to compile a list of the fifty people who made Scotland great you'd end up with some historian going: 'Erm, was he a Viking? I can't remember. Oh, and there was this other guy, but he was English, I think . . .' Whereas, you try to summon fifty people who fucked the country and you're spoilt for choice. Failure and disappointment are the best ways in which to consider Scotland's history. We are much happier counting our sorrows than our blessings. Scotland really is a place where the loch is half-empty not half-full.

In this spirit, I was disappointed not to be on the list myself. Everyone who ever left Scotland should be on it; Ronald McDonald even. There are few politicians on it, I notice, which is sensible because democracy is completely wasted on the Scots. The place doesn't have politics, it has tribalism. Almost everyone you meet here will tell you they were born to put their X in a certain box on the ballot paper, no matter what. So, oddly, the only properly democratic choice anyone ever makes in Scotland is to vote Conservative, which is the one persuasion Scots aren't born into.

There are other omissions. John Knox, for example, who I think embodies a whole strain of Scottishness which is incredibly misogynistic, which despises and hates and mistrusts women, and having fun. Picture Knox and you see those drippy-nosed, sour, prune-faced churchmen in Edinburgh and you think, You are all the children of John Knox. It is very amusing, and very Scottish, and very telling, that Macbeth isn't on the list either; the one proper international baddy we own. Not even to include his wife! I gather the nationalists are trying to redefine Macbeth at the moment, so it's a complex issue. But, then, for the Scots, even Lulu is a complex issue.

The worst thing about Scotland, really, is that old truism (everything about Scotland is an old truism), that point about Celts in general. We are absolutely the end of the line. There be homo sapiens, the Neanderthals and then there are Celts. You just feel we are dying out. We're *almost* the same as everyone else but there's something slightly different about us. We're the bit at the end, on this fringe of islands in the north. We used to be all over Europe and all over Asia and now we're stuck in a couple of bothies on Skye. We're becoming extinct and endangered; we're the orang-utans of the north.

Scotland has always suffered from the humour of its malevolent gods, who stuck us next to the English. In a sense, the defining nature of Scotland has always been England. Scotland has a song-and-dance for a culture, and don't we make a song and dance of the fact? We've spent hundreds of years saying how not English we are. Scotland is happier measuring its woes and telling the world what it's not – we're not southern, we're not poncy, we're not snobby, we're not epicurean – but, most of all, we're not English. The Irish and the Welsh do this too, of course, but hardly to the same extent. Scotland is a country defined by what it isn't. And it seldom tells us what it actually is. Scotland should have been the country that invented Elastoplast; we're constantly bandaged from self-inflicted wounds, from having walked into low doors and tripped over other people's feet.

All that said, one point more than any other needs to be made about Scotland: that it is great despite itself. Scotland is still, if you have any connection to the place at all – even if you're a Dutchman who wants to come and shoot things once a year – far and away the greatest place in the world. It's just difficult to say why. There is a mixture of people and landscape and air and light and culture and dry wit and deep intelligence and enquiry and disappointment and maudlinness and lyricism that go together to make Scotland utterly exceptional. However, its greatest sons either left or fucked-up, and those who stayed behind are about as useful as broken tumble-dryers. Let's meet them.

A.A. Gill, London

Introduction

The other evening while flicking through the channels I chanced upon an episode of *Cracker*, the one with the serial killer who forces his victims to dress up as Shirley Temple; a particular favourite, it pains me to say. The scene featured a funeral, where the arrival of the coffin was accompanied by a choirboy singing a verse of 'The Bonnie Banks of Loch Lomond'. He fluted away winsomely, outlining in song the sundry advantages of taking the high road over taking low road and so forth. I looked on impassively. Then something curious occurred. A tear leaked slowly from the corner of my right eye. A big, hot tear. Weird.

Or perhaps not. This is the double bind of the Scottish experience. The hooks and barbs seem to enter at the most tender point. To be Scottish means always to be at the mercy of this stuff and to carry round a headful of it: the fading Polaroids of memory, the sporran fluff of sentiment. Scottish wistfulness, I've found, has a sweet and plangent quality, like finding a crumpled Wombles poster in a seldom-explored cupboard. So much of the nation's culture was blithe, cartoonish and quaint to begin with that the passage of time only renders it more disarming yet.

Most Scots, I'd suggest, hold in their minds a photomontage of these quaint glories. On my own montage, a CalMac ferry forever ploughs towards some misty little isle. On Loch Lomond, the

1940s post boat is doing its rounds. There is the particular look of the settlements as you leave the central belt and each mile travelled north takes you a year back in time, to storybook villages where old blokes are forever painting benches British racing green. There's a view of Crinan in Argyllshire, where a horseshoe of mountains encloses a loch of glassy stillness, with a fishing skip in the middle, as though placed there by God to give a sense of scale. Fleeting, doomed Scottish pop stars and forgotten footballers feature too, facing down their dismalness. The bobble-hatted explorer Tom Weir makes an appearance, gnawing his way through an inexhaustible slab of Kendal Mint Cake. There are advertisements for Scottish concerns long since vanished: Agnew's Off-Licence, Creamola Foam, Solripe soft drinks. There is the Loch Ness monster, the otter, the wildcat. All of it is rendered in the nostalgic, heartbreaking hues of an old seaside postcard.

My montage, then, is really quite pleasant, a vision of a Scotland that is cosy and harmless, a land of cheerful anachronism and measured optimism. Having said that, it is quite easy also to loathe the bloody place. Viewed without the filters of sentiment, modern Scotland is unremittingly grim, really quite frightful. A deep seam of defeat runs in the national soul. The population, in the main, is coarse, badly educated and poorly spoken. Wit is considered indicative of flaming homosexuality and replaced with punchlines. The skies are the colour of a week-old bandage. The cities resemble architectural suicide notes, being mainly shoeboxes built from granite. The national diet would scandalise a feral child. Alcohol is abused fiercely, proudly even. By default it is assumed that nothing can or will improve. Politics won't help; loyalties are split between ineffectual, discredited Scottish Labour and the nationalists, as windy as a night on Ben Nevis. Comfort is sought in sport, but seldom found.

Taken together, these contingencies are not easy to withstand. There is but one recourse, to an ongoing untruth, to a collective lie; a lie which insists, despite all evidence to the contrary, that Scotland is the greatest small nation on earth, a wise, kind, judicious, compassionate, big-hearted and welcoming place, rich in pride, myth and legend, but done down by envy and conspiracy, by misfortunes it has done nothing to earn. One aspect of the problem was implied in *The Fall of Kelvin Walker*, Alasdair Gray's wickedly funny novel in which a Presbyterian innocent makes his way in Swinging London: 'Money seemed a slower substance in the north – a powerful substance, certainly, but stolid,' wrote Gray. 'Those owning it had not been liberated by it. Their faces were as severe, their mouths as grimly clenched as those without. But here in London money had accumulated to a point where it had flashed into wealth, and wealth was free, swift, reckless, mercuric. He could feel it humming behind the ancient and modern facades, throbbing under the streets like silver-electric sap.' This about sums it up, captures the importance Scots place upon their own misery, and on the impossibility of change. The poem 'Scotland' by Alasdair Reid (Scottish history features a good number of Alasdairs) touches on it too, when the author remarks to a passer-by on the pleasantness of the weather: 'Her brow grew bleak, her ancestors raged in their ancient graves/As she spoke with their ancient misery: We'll pay for it, we'll pay for it, we'll pay for it!'

As Reid indicates, the mindset stretches way back into the nation's history. To be Scottish is to hear repeatedly, in history, culture and society, the phrase 'And then it got worse.' Here, failure is a cosmic inevitability. The birthright of Scotland is not glory but entropy. Little improves. Some Scots of certain political persuasions will argue this is not our fault, that others have done us down, because they envy our ingenuity or our hardiness or our solidarity or our comity. This is wishful thinking. The truth is that there is a disability in the Scottish soul, an inherent glumness or vainglory, which became circular. The story of Scotland is the story of a snake consuming its own tail then discovering it has heartburn. The Scots never quite get it right. Something in the very air, the soil, the history, the thinking or the mindset conspires to confound us.

To look at the history of Scotland, then, is to marvel that a country of five million people could prove itself so inept and of such little consequence (that noise you hear in the distance may be Scottish nationalists, screaming about John Logie Baird). The inherent caution and fatalism described previously have conspired to paralyse. Those with any amount of talent or foresight depart as early as possible, usually to London, by tradition a Promised Land to the Scot. Arriving there is when they realise their lives have passed in being fibbed to. The experience of London is baptismal. Reactions become faster, references become broader. Life is revealed to be more volatile and various than it ever could be in damp old Scotia. The Scottish cream goes there, and leaves behind it a residue of the watery UHT. I cannot exclude myself from this; it is the greatest regret of my life that I didn't get out twenty years ago.

Much of this UHT is considered here. Seen in the mass we understand something about the hollowness of the Scottish experience. It is a land that has gone centuries without those two engines of social vitality, church and government; or, rather, without any versions of these that have commanded much popular respect; comprising in the first instance the derided ('Ask an Edinburgh prostitute when is Christmas,' went an old Billy Connolly routine. 'She'll say, "When's the General Synod of the Church of Scotland?"') or, in the second, of mere technocratic administrators. There is myth and legend but none of the deep, quiet connection with tradition found in Wales, say. There isn't even a geographic unit we could call Scotland; just Glasgow, Edinburgh and some far-flung branch offices in Aberdeen, Dundee and Inverness. This is a nation where the largest city, Glasgow, laughs at all the others, considering them sleepy and rather backward.

With what is Scotland left? With bad ambassadors, really, as discussed on the pages that follow. The nation is left with characters who move through the world tarnishing further the family silver. To be Scottish is to have a lot to live down and this lot do the job superbly, whether this be Robert Burns, indecipherable bard of rustic gibberish; Bonnie Prince Charlie, lisping midget mercenary; Sir Arthur Conan Doyle, the blithering populariser of spiritualism; Sean Connery, die-hard advocate of a country he refuses to live in; or Billy Connolly, punchable *faux*-prole. In the realm of politics there are Kenny MacAskill, the SNP minister who converted Scotland's biggest break on the global stage into cringing horror; Alex Salmond, the chortling bullfrog of separatism; the insufferable George Galloway, member of parliament for the West Bank; Tommy Sheridan, the sexy socialist who lent new meaning to the term hardliner. They're all here, sadly. And many others; a veritable embassy of bad ambassadors.

Allan Brown, Glasgow

Stuart Adamson

n a corner of rural Fife sits a rock 'n' roll hotel. Of a sort. It's not the Chateau Marmont or any suchlike; you won't find there the great and good of Scottish popular music – Barbara Dickson, say, or Susan Boyle – ingesting speedballs and ordering camels from room service. This place is more restrained. Superannuated heritage acts – Pentangle, perhaps, or some old super-competent folk guitarist – trundle up in their SUVs, stay a few days, play some mellow acoustic sets, head off to St Andrews for a round of golf and generally have a very pleasant and amply-cashmered time of it.

Meanwhile, the hotel's rooms are themed in honour of various renowned Scottish rock and pop names, with gold discs on display and autographed memorabilia. Among the performers honoured is Stuart Adamson, guitarist and bandleader, initially of The Skids, most famously of Big Country. Sadly, in 2001 Adamson, deep in despair and estranged from his wife, hanged himself, in Hawaii, in a hotel room. Should you ever check into the Lathones Inn you too may find yourself in the Stuart Adamson suite. To sleep in a room dedicated to a man who despatched himself in just such a place is a disquieting experience; akin to dining at the Karen Carpenter Sandwich Bar, or travelling in a model of luxury saloon named for Princess Diana.

Such is what early and tragic death does for an entertainer: it shrouds them in gold leaf. Had James Dean lived, by now he'd be just another tanned robot king of mid-afternoon American television. Brian Jones of The Rolling Stones would have faded to insignificance. Instead, each has entered the halls of hallowed memory. Something similar has occurred with Adamson. Yearly, his reputation grows, even if his contribution and legacy are of genuinely arguable merit.

This is not to argue Big Country were not successful. They were. Their album *Steeltown* went to number one in October 1984; two years later *The Seer* almost repeated the feat. The band enjoyed a clutch of hit singles: 'Fields of Fire', 'In a Big Country', 'Chance', 'Look Away'. For five years they competed respectably at the upper levels of British rock, falling into step with the contemporaneous fad for expressive, heartfelt rock from the Celtic fringes, as practiced also by U2, Simple Minds, The Waterboys and Hothouse Flowers.

Which is where the problems began. Few in their proper mind ever found the Celtic fringe anything but hilarious. As a genre, whether in music or literature, it was neither sophisticated, elegant nor evolved. It was culture with smallholdings in its head. It prioritised none of the virtues that informed the great efflorescence of cultural and philosophical thought in the post-medieval British mainstream, from Chaucer to Larkin via Dr Samuel Johnson. Rather, the Celtic tradition was bosky and windswept, animistic and pagan, agricultural and druidic. It was gnobbly, gnarly and it didn't wipe its feet at the door. It was a yokelish Yeatsian knees-up. It concerned itself with the elemental; the changing of the seasons, the soul, feelings, meteorological phenomena and religiose intensity. It was the equivalent of a freckled, red-haired forearm hooking round your throat and insisting with eighty-proof breath you share with its owner some of your *craic*.

But it had its day. The Celtic fringe started percolating into the musical bloodstream in the 1960s through the folk revival, then through Van Morrison, Rory Gallagher, Horslips and U2. By the time of Big Country the trend was in full spate. The Scottish band, however, had not the wit to contribute in anything but the least inspiring of fashions. Like the Bay City Rollers, they adopted tartan; or rather plaid, wearing their shirts open-necked and with roughly-tied neckerchiefs that connoted a hard day picking turnips. And they developed a notorious musical trademark: guitars that sounded like bagpipes. This was achieved with a certain vile ingenuity. When Adamson played a solo he did so on the thinnest strings and high up the neck, in order that the note was brittle and piercing. His riffs would approximate the limited tonal scale of wind instrumentation: short intervals, no flurries of notes, no bending of strings. Typically, the phrase was doubled up by a second guitarist, playing marginally out of phase, both using effect pedals that accentuated this keening, otherworldly air. To this day, the very idea of guitars made to sound like bagpipes is associated uniquely and indelibly with Stuart Adamson. He remains for evermore the guitars-like-bagpipes guy.

Behind this predilection were mitigating circumstances. The early 1980s were a querulous time in British culture. Several years earlier, punk had functioned as a kind of disruption, a year zero. The curtain was torn away to expose at the culture's core a middle-aged, suburban bankruptcy. Music was suffering, as would be confirmed by anyone who'd witnessed the long-haired fret-stranglers on *The Old Grey Whistle Test*. Television was ruled by a cast of misfits: Bob Harris, Jimmy Savile, Mike Yarwood, Benny Hill, Noele Gordon on *Crossroads*, Roy Castle, Larry Grayson *et al.*

As the 1980s progressed a mood grew for something more organic, more sincere. Britain in the early 1980s felt as though it were coming round from a concussion, pained that during its incapacity matters had grown so parlous. Music led the recovery. New influences started creeping in: world music via Talking Heads, electronica via Kraftwerk and The Human League; and, most consequentially, in commercial terms at least, Celtic rock, as reminted by U2. That band had issued its debut album in October, 1980, almost precisely the period during which Adamson left The Skids, the art-rock band with which he'd had several hit singles, most notably 'Into the Valley'. For musicians raised in Scotland and southern Ireland opening up was a new avenue of operation; of anthemic, power-ballad folk-rock that sang of quests and struggles and flame-haired colleens washing clothes in the river; a music of mountains, sorrow and lobster pots.

Adamson clearly sensed this change in the wind's direction and, like a wily trawlerman, he capitalised upon it. Which was fair enough. Celtic rock was not devoid wholly of merit: The Waterboys, for example, made a number of excellent records. The problem lay in the fact that Adamson's *version* of Celtic rock was so poor in itself, so lumpen and lamentable, so Scottish in its literal way. When a Big Country number approached its crescendo and required an exclamation point Adamson would bark 'Ha!' like a sergeant- major drilling recruits. The lyrics appeared to be drawn wholly from the Bumper Book of Post-Culloden Woe, full of men gazing nobly into the middle distance as their jaws resisted the urge to tremble. Sporadically the band would slip into martial tempo. Their songs had portentous titles that made you want to punch the nearest dog: 'The Seer', 'The Teacher', 'Broken Heart (Thirteen Valleys)'. It was lowest-common-denominator stuff, stripped of wit, nuance, sex and subtlety. It was fodder, servicing a fad and nothing more. You perused a Big Country audience and had one thought: if all these people are *here*, who's manning the city's filling stations?

Clearly, the entire Big Country ethos had been bolted together to appeal to audiences in North America, where U2 had so parlayed into dollars and cents similar auld-world sincerity and misty, mossy race memory. Addressing this, the band's name evoked – cleverly, it must be conceded – both the Highlands of Scotland and the prairies of the American west. The fullness of time, however, revealed Big Country to be second-raters, and Adamson something of an opportunist, swathing his music in Highland drag. We can't really criticise him for what he failed to do. Let us focus, instead, upon what he did do, which was to whittle the big knobbly stick with which Scottish rock music would henceforth be beaten, rendering Scottish music a novelty, every bit as effectively as Andy Stewart had with 'Donald Where's Yer Troosers?' Adamson helped foster a kind of comedy cartoon rock, *Brigadoon* with drums, a hot porridge enema. At least he received a fitting memorial.

Wendy Alexander

Wendy Alexander shouldn't be in this company, not really. The former MSP wasn't *that* bad; she wasn't George Galloway bad. But she did table a bad amendment, in support of a project that became perhaps the most vivid nightmare in Scottish civic history. In arguing for the reintroduction of trams to Edinburgh, Alexander wasn't to know things would pan out so calamitously. Nor was she to know that when the lights were switched on finally the cockroaches would scatter so effectively for the security of the skirting board. The tram fiasco, in which a £276m spend ballooned to a projected £1 billion (probably to rise further), was a crime scene without fingerprints, a vast capital project overseen by the unknown and the unseen, by massed Kafkaesque ranks of council committees and incompetent contractors. The dust is settling still, but amid the wreckage lies most conspicuously the parliamentary record of the fateful advocacy of Scottish Labour, and, particularly, of Wendy Alexander.

This not to say that Alexander, trams apart, had not faults in her own right. During her political career she was well known as a forthright and bustling irritant; a nippy sweetie, albeit one with a solid record in formulating business strategy. As the old Scottish saying had it, she was not a woman to confront with a half-spent pay packet. Diminutive, power-suited and Jagger-gobbed,

Alexander was strident, a student-union placard in sling-backs. She was one thing above all others: a Labour devotee. One could imagine easily the bedroom of her teenage years, its walls covered in heart-throb posters of Keir Hardie and Harold Wilson. Such sense of purpose occasioned an impressive rise, from management consultancy to special adviser to Donald Dewar in his tenure as Secretary for State for Scotland, then on to Holyrood as MSP, Minister and, briefly, leader of Scottish Labour.

But this sense of purpose engendered also, perhaps, a sense of hubris, seen *nonpareil* when she told an interviewer Labour had little to fear from an independence referendum and urged the nationalists to 'bring it on', an incitement that earned her a smack-down from close ally Gordon Brown. Greater discomfort was to follow. In 2007 Alexander's campaign for the forthcoming Holyrood election accepted a £950 donation from a party sup-porter based in Jersey. The benefactor was not registered to vote in UK elections, rendering his donation illegal. Alexander cited sundry mitigating technicalities but to no avail and in June 2008 she was forced, by the 'vexatious' efforts of the SNP, she claimed, to resign, less than a year since taking office.

So, a party girl, in the least scintillating sense of the term; a megaphone for the official line. Very much the Alexander who in June 2007 told Parliament, regarding the stuttering tram project: 'The Minister for Transport [Stewart Stevenson of the SNP] claimed that the costs were out of control, but they are not.' The Edinburgh trams project had been a runaway nightmare since 1998 when Professor Lewis Lesley of John Moore's University (and tram entrepreneur) put to Edinburgh council an idea for a tram-line running from Haymarket in the city centre to Newhaven, a waterfront area two miles north. A public consultation was favourable. In the minds of councillors the idea began to take hold. In 2002, Transport Initiative Edinburgh was established, operated by transport-industry professionals and former councillors. At the time the Scottish executive was a Labour/Lib Dem coalition for which the notion of a tram system ticked several boxes, being a job-creating capital expenditure project that offered environmental benefits and a touch of continental *élan*. A budget was set: £500 million from the Parliament, £45 million from City of Edinburgh Council. It all seemed so swizzy, so post-fossil fuel.

In May 2007, however, the Lib/Lab coalition was replaced by a minority SNP government. From the outset the SNP, proving that a stopped clock is correct at least twice a day, had opposed the tram plan; too pricey, too Labourite. It moved to have the scheme scrapped. The issue came to the chamber at the end of June, 2007. It was touch and go. Alexander said the SNP objection was one that 'oozes with party prejudice and geographic grudge'. She argued passionately for Edinburgh's trams. Yes, she added, there was a need for fiscal responsibility and the observance of budgetary limitations. But the trams had to go ahead. She carried the day, eighty-one votes to forty-seven. The trams were go. Or not, as it transpired.

Matters stepped up a gear, if indeed trams have gears. Alexander's budgetary limits meant it was not possible for the line to run from Haymarket to Granton, which had sort of been the point of the thing. All that could be afforded was an eleven-mile stretch from Newhaven to Edinburgh Airport, via Princes Street. Eyebrows were raised at the sourcing of components: tracks forged in Vienna, overhead lines and ticketing technology by Siemens of Germany, tramcars built in Spain. When city streets began to be closed off and dug up headlines got worse by the day: Tram Chiefs Admit We Have No Idea What Final Bill Will Be; Shambolic Tram Project is up to Two Years Behind; Half of Staff Facing Axe at

Troubled Tram Firm; Traders Unhappy as Shandwick Place to Close for 18 Months; Edinburgh's Tram Tracks to Need Repairs BEFORE They Have Even Been Used. It was revealed householders along the route would need permission before washing their windows to avoid the hazards of overhead power cables. A UN environmental committee considered complaints that trams were causing pollution by diverting traffic along residential streets. Good news was there none. Ever. Back in October 2007 the agencies involved had promised that the first day of tram operation would be 25 February 2011. On the day in question, 72 per cent of construction work remained, and just 38 per cent of budget.

Why did all this happen? Those of an apocalyptic mindset would argue it couldn't have gone any other way given it was happening in Scotland, a nation of almost cosmic incompetence in handling major public projects. It remains impossible to credit that such a transformative undertaking in such an architecturally sensitive city was delegated to designers and engineers who had no acquaintance with the place. Everyday contingencies played their parts too: the standard comings and goings of personnel from boards and companies; the scepticism of press and public; engineering difficulties. It could all have been so different had the plan gone no further, had a certain MSP kept her counsel one afternoon in June 2007, and in doing so denied the SNP a propaganda victory whose benefits it continues to reap; an MSP by the name of Wendy Alexander.

The Bay City Rollers

Of all the names associated with Greek tragedy, and particularly with its defining precepts of Destiny, Hubris and Nemesis, The Bay City Rollers never quite ranked with Aeschylus and Sophocles. Nothing about the band was redolent of the higher functions. Its constituency was humbler, mainly adolescents named Karen and Donna urinating over the tip-up seats of their local Hippodrome.

You will scarcely need reminding that the group from Edinburgh was hugely and globally successful, selling during its brief combustion around one hundred million records. But Rollermania was a craze of a certain hollow kind. Rewind fifty years. When Beatlemania subsided, it matured into a deeper and more considered appreciation of its object, The Beatles. Such, however, did not happen with the Rollers. The hysteria surrounding the band was brief and swiftly regretted. And once it was over those who'd been affected, whether performer or fan, sported expressions of dazed disappointment, like someone realising the apple they'd been given by the stage hypnotist was, in fact, an onion.

The Roller tragedy was of two kinds: personal and general. For the members themselves, for Les, Alan, Derek, Eric and Woody, there was, as noted, destiny, hubris and nemesis; the rocketing ascent and dying fall of all teenybop bands. The Rollers had it all, then awoke to discover they didn't. This was bad enough. But the dismay was sharpened fiendishly, by fiscal chicanery of quite astonishing dimensions, that obliged the former members to spend over three decades suffering court proceedings of Dickensian complexity, in order to retrieve the missing £5 billion in profits.

The second tragedy was greater yet, for it touched every Scot. It was that the nation's biggest-ever pop sensation, its conquering heroes, turned out at heart to be such a seedy and morally squalid gaggle of ne'er-do-wells. This did not happen with, say, the Swedes. So far as we know, Benny and Björn of Abba did not knock down and kill any old-age pensioners. Anni-Frid and Agnetha side-stepped any claim they'd deployed an air rifle to shoot at their own fans. Slade, The Sweet and Gilbert O'Sullivan dodged the nightmares of drug abuse and paedophilia.

Not the Rollers, though. The band's hour in the sun had been spent purveying the musical equivalent of Valentine's cards but at heart the five were darker than death metal. Take vocalist Les McKeown. Eleven years ago, when McKeown published his auto-biography, *Shang-a-Lang*, the book's subtitle was *Life as an International Pop Idol*. The book was reissued in 2006 and its subtitle was amended: to *The Curse of the Bay City Rollers*. For their brace of golden years the band paid the heftiest of prices, from heart attacks, strokes, child porn convictions and fatal road accidents to bankruptcy, poverty and mutual loathing. When things started going wrong for the Bay City Rollers they didn't stop. Or as their entry in the *Encyclopedia of Popular Music* puts it: 'Disaster was heaped upon disaster.'

The band was formed by brothers Derek and Alan Longmuir in the late 1960s, as a Beatles covers outfit. An entrepreneur, Tam Paton, moulded the teenagers into a quasi-novelty act, doe-eyed and plaid-clad, while staff writers furnished them with a stream of upbeat, soppy ballads: 'Give a Little Love', 'Shang-a-Lang', 'All of Me Loves All of You'. The formula caught fire in America and Japan too.

And then McKeown hit a 76-year-old Edinburgh woman with his turbo-charged Ford Mustang 351 and killed her. His conviction for reckless driving was the band's death knell. Soon he had been fired from the Rollers, for raising objections to a Rollers TV show for kids; then he had his house repossessed. The band split up. Court battles for the Rollers' name and royalties began.

In 1982 Paton received a three-year sentence for gross indecency against two teenage boys. In 2004 he was fined £200,000 for supplying cannabis. He suffered a stroke after being cleared of further child abuse allegations. Alan Longmuir had a heart attack and a stroke and took a job as as a plumber in Bannockburn. His brother Derek, a psychiatric nurse, was convicted of downloading child porn. Little was heard of guitarist Eric Faulkner or Stuart 'Woody' Wood beyond their involvement in various Roller revival projects. In 2005, McKeown was acquitted of conspiracy to supply cocaine.

The band still performs on the nostalgia circuit but in two versions: one with McKeown and one without. Legal actions are fired off sporadically like distress flares, to establish rights to the band's name or to have its former manager arrested for sexually abusing a stand-in guitarist. There are sporadic salvos in that legal monster of a case, towards clawing back the millions in royalties the members believe was misappropriated by their record company, which, conveniently, dissolved long ago. It can be only a matter of time before a member sues himself by accident.

The Rollers were well-scrubbed lads of questionable versatility, brought together at a time when only managers and producers knew where the money really went. They neither wrote nor played on most of their hits; only sentiment of the gloopiest kind was permitted. Which explains why roughly 800 women in their mid-forties have descended on Croydon tonight. Songs such as *Shang-a-Lang*, *Summerlove Sensation* and *Bye Bye Baby* were hokey and threadbare even when first released. Three decades later they have to be eked out with modern rock and reggae passages. At £15 per ticket, the performance struggles to last the hour. If Friends Reunited held concerts they would be like this; self-conscious restagings of simpler times, replete with mock-ironic screams and joke-lust grabs at the singer. It's the female equivalent of watching a veterans' football squad; a half-sad, half-serious pantomime. When Les McKeown's Legendary Bay City Rollers come to town, even the inverted commas have inverted commas.

Backstage afterwards, McKeown is something of a mess, wired and croaky, still high from the adrenaline of the show but never shaking off his deep bass note of dejection. Earning a living aside, he must really hate all this, churning out the same old riffs for the same old riffraff, knowing his millions remain on the other side of yet further legal battles, ceaselessly recycling songs that were never much good in the first place. In 2006, he says, he received a back-dated royalty cheque for £900,000 but was unable to cash it until some ancient arcane contractual matter had been resolved among his former colleagues. It hasn't been yet, and a further sum, allegedly £50 million, is caught in a similar fankle.

McKeown says that if it eventually comes through he will give most of it to charity. He needs money, he says, only for alcohol, cigarettes and his family. He is striving to foster a philosophical perspective, disattached from greed and ego. Energetic positivity, he believes, will turn things around. 'The fans are reviving their childhood thing,' he says sadly. 'I've got to respect that and come to terms with that. I'm stuck in the pigeonhole of the Bay City Rollers. I don't like being stuck in it, but I am.'

Does he wish the Bay City Rollers had never happened? Not at all, he says. He could have been in a better band, he says, a cooler band, but this is his life and he's trying to make the best of it. 'I'm relatively happy, trying to make it through the world,' he says. 'All this stuff happens in everyone's life. You get creditors coming after you, the council tax people. Everybody suffers. That's the way I have to look at it. I don't suffer in a different way just because I'm famous.' Besides, between nostalgia tours, his new band keeps him busy. McKeown doesn't sing in this band, he just plays guitar. The band is called Damaged.

Alexander Graham Bell

niquely amongst civilised nations, the Scots have learnt their national history not from a song or an epic poem but from a souvenir tea-towel. You might recall the towel in question. It was always on sale in the gift shops and keepsake caves we encountered on childhood holidays to Mull and Millport. It depicted a *tableau vivant* in which frock-coated, full-bearded gents went about devising the objects that would commend them to history. Here, for instance, John Logie Baird was refining television as James Chalmers created the postage stamp. Over there, Charles Macintosh was fashioning the raincoat and, later, Alexander Fleming was synthesising penicillin. This tea-towel was like a GCSE in 75 per cent Terylene. By stealth, sneakily as we dried the crockery, was inculcated a suspicion that Scots were Special Ones, a golden race, one that created, invented, forged and wiped the mud off absolutely everything there had ever been, with the possible exception of Morris dancing, which the English were welcome to.

The real truth of Scottish history, the hairy, thistly and knobbly truth, is more nuanced, obviously. As much went wrong as ever went right. Or, rather, that alongside each glorious achievement was a sinister *doppelgänger*, a Hyde of horror who shadowed the Jekylls of joy. In the modern age, it has become clear that a particular type of misfortune is very much Scotland's birthright; a mordant kind, where reality thwarts and disappoints the Scots in fiendish and ingenious ways; where tartan rugs are pulled from beneath unsuspecting hiking boots. And so the nation has a dual history: one in which great patriots perform heroic deeds, and a second one in which, for some inexplicable reason, things seem repeatedly to fall on their sides.

Alexander Graham Bell demonstrates the paradox beautifully. Ask any schoolchild about Bell and they will tell you confidently: he was the Edinburgh-born engineer who came up with the idea of the telephone. A different answer, though, will be provided by those with any knowledge of the history of the invention of the device. Enquire of any such person the identity of Alexander Graham Bell and there is every chance they will splutter, mumble, then direct your attention towards a passing kestrel. For Bell was Scotland's great fib, a skeleton in a cupboard. He invented the telephone in the way Jack the Ripper invented modern policing. Which is to say, he didn't; he merely became embroiled in a process that was occurring anyway. It's perfectly understandable that Scotland would wish to claim as its own the man who devised arguably the single most consequential invention since the wheel. However, the way in which Scotland set about doing so is shifty, albeit crucial in the growth of the nation's inflated sense of itself. Bell was the thin end of the wedge. Bell put the worm in the bud. All bets were off. The lie had been cast.

As anyone who has watched *The Godfather III* knows, the inventor of the telephone was one Antonio Meucci. In the gangster melodrama, hoodlum Joey Zasa presents Michael Corleone with a Man of the Year award on behalf of the Meucci Association, a fictional body honouring the Italian-American folk hero: 'He invented the telephone one year before Alexander Graham Bell,' Zasa tells the Godfather. The dates were less than accurate, even if those in the know were scarcely queuing up to correct the psychotic murderer. In fact, Meucci arrived at the telephone five years earlier than Bell. The problem was that on the patent application Meucci fell foul of a technicality, by failing to mention the device was not mechanical or acoustic in nature but electromagnetic. Five years later, in 1876, Bell would fail to make the same mistake. Paperwork completed satisfactorily, Bell went on to win the garlands, even if it took several decades for the garlands to be thrown. The evidence suggests that Bell had scant understanding of what he had 'created'. He has gone into history for predicting, somewhat gormlessly, that 'one day every major city in America will have a telephone'.

Let's not write the old boy off completely. Bell deserves some acknowledgement as at least a telephonic pioneer. Just not as a telephonic inventor. It is all a question of intention. Inarguably, Meucci set out to devise a device that did what telephones do, for the purposes we associate now with telephone function. He had a background in theatre and at one point required a means of communication between the stage and the control room. Later, in America, when his wife Ester was diagnosed with rheumatoid arthritis, Meucci had need of a connection between her bedroom and his laboratory. Made wealthy by his innovations in water purification, his greatest passion was the electromagnetic transmission. In 1856, he built a prototype 'talking telegraph' and refined it with thirty successive models. When it came to inventing the telephone, then, Meucci, as his dubious advocates among the Italian-American criminal sodality would have put it, had the motive, the means and the opportunity.

Bell, on the other hand, came from a family of elocution teachers; his interest was more the mechanics of speech than its transmission. To this end, he devised an experiment upon the family West Highland terrier in which the dog was taught to growl continuously while Bell reached into its mouth to manipulate its lips and vocal cords, achieving eventually an approximate rendering of the phrase 'How are you, mama?'. Let this notion stay briefly in your mind. A venture even creepier was a machine titled the phonautograph that resonated membranes in an ear procured from a corpse. Further developments followed: like the Harmonic Telegraph, which sent several Morse code messages simultaneously; and one named the Gallows, that transmitted not speech but voice-like sounds. Paydirt was hit, though, with a machine that caused a needle to vibrate in a container of water, thus varying the resistance in an electrical circuit. The device possessed clearly the necessary electromagnetic component. In New York, meanwhile, Meucci was attempting to patent his more straightforward device. Had he done so in an acceptable manner there is every possibility we would never again have heard from Bell. In 2002 the US Patents Office conceded that had proper procedure been followed at the time, the patent for the electromagnetic transmission of vocal sound by undulatory electric current would have gone to Meucci. Bell's claim to his place on Scotland's ye olde souvenir tea-towel was exposed finally as dubious. And those who would disagree are invited to press their complaint by contacting The Mafia, c/o Little Italy, New York.

Bonnie Prince Charlie

In the Scottish psyche no word clangs so grimly as Culloden. The name is a depressing interloper each time it is heard, a synonym for defeat, despair and humiliation. This is so even when you break the word to its constituent parts: yielding *cull* as in slaughter, and *oden*, suggestive of some mystical northern being, watching from on high as Scottish blood stains the soil.

This is pretty much what happened there: a vicious, shin-kicking rammy in 1746, on a bleak moor near Inverness, in which soldiers fighting for the restoration of a Stuart monarchy were routed by government troops led by William Augustus, Duke of Cumberland. Culloden was David and Goliath in the Highlands. Our image of Culloden comes mainly from Morier's painting, showing the soldiers in their uniforms of vibrant red raining bayonets upon a shabby gaggle of plaid-clad clansmen. We think of the battle as epic, a long week's tussle for the soul of Scotland. In fact, it lasted less than an hour, so paltry was the Jacobite opposition. On the side of the Jacobite aggressors, two thousand were killed, compared with fifty Englishmen.

And, essentially, it was all the fault of Bonnie Prince Charlie; aka Charles Edward Stuart, the Young Pretender, or one of them. Can ever a bloodier outcome have been the doing of such a frivolous, insubstantial man? Surely not. Looking at the bonnie

prince is like discovering Larry Grayson caused the Blitz. There is a deep disjunction between the man and his legacy. He gave us perhaps the most bloody and dismal episode in Scottish history, all the while wondering if the ribbons on his shoes complemented his eyes.

Hence, almost three centuries after Charlie snuck out the side door of history, wearing a large hat and a bushy moustache, he remains a folkloric pop star. Restaurants and bars bear his name. His graven image is seen from Lockerbie to Wick; he is disliked in the south of Scotland, for reasons we shall return to. He is on the Mount Rushmore of Scottishness, alongside Billy Connolly, Sean Connery, Sir Harry Lauder and *Braveheart*. If a movie version of Culloden were made in the modern day, Charlie would be central to all the bits that made it into the trailer: his landing at Eriskay; the raising of the standard at Glenfinnan, where he swore lustily he'd reclaim the crown for his exiled father, James Stewart; his armed incursion into England; Culloden itself, and the subsequent chase sequence across the Hebrides as Charlie fled the English. There'd even a catchy theme tune, 'The Skye Boat Song', and a romantic sub-plot starring the sultry Flora Macdonald.

When the legend becomes fact, says someone in *The Man Who Shot Liberty Valance*, print the legend. Few have benefited from this injunction as Bonnie Prince Charlie has. The legend has it that when he landed at Eriskay, following a botched departure from France, Charlie encountered a local chieftain who instructed him to go home. *I am home*, he replied. Ever since, history has begged leave to doubt him. The good son bit was a red herring. It wasn't all in the name of the father. It is thought Charlie's project was, in essence, diversionary, a French-sponsored ruse to tie up British ships and soldiers and render their counterparts in southerly climes vulnerable to attack. It was a singularly Gallic raspberry blown in the face of perfidious Albion, something for *les rosbifs* to chew on. Scotland was merely the location, rather than the focus, of Charlie's activities.

Yet Charlie remains a romantic hero, demonstrating to us that Culloden is woefully misunderstood still. We regard him as a Scarlet Pimpernel figure, as dashing, brave and restless. In fact, he was cowardly and inept. In the movies that dramatise the battle, *Culloden* and *Chasing The Deer*, he is scarcely to be seen. He is remembered fondly because he was the underdog, a category for which the Scots retain a default sympathy, regardless of the particularities. Scotland supports underdogs unfailingly, on a point of general principle, no doubt because the nation has so often found itself in the underdog role itself. The continuing cult of Bonnie Prince Charlie is taken as a sign that Scotland does not forget those who fight for her interests. What it shows really is the basic lack of understanding most Scots possess about their own history.

Jimmy Boyle

ave you, perchance, been to East Kilbride? Hardly an enquiry
to get the pulse racing, we know, but sincere nonetheless.
Lying eight miles south of Glasgow, East Kilbride is a decent and
unremarkable settlement. It was built in the late 1940s, part of the
post-war dust-down, as an overspill from the congested and crumbling urban centre. On the draughtsman's drawing board East
Kilbride was planned to be pleasant, spacious and verdant. And so
it was, certainly to begin with. To weary and brutalised Glaswegians
the new town represented nothing so much as a new beginning, a
phoenix from the ashes of the broken city.

This did not mean the past had been forgotten, not completely.
This was demonstrated in 1999, when Jimmy Boyle came a-calling.
Then as now, Boyle was a well-kent figure. In Glasgow's east end in
the 1960s he'd been a moneylender, hoodlum and, in time, a
convicted murderer. Duly, he became a prisoner, a notoriously
violent one, spirited round Scotland's jails like the bird of ill-omen.
He ended up at Barlinnie Prison in Glasgow, where, as luck would
have it, a radical programme in prisoner rehabilitation was being
trialled, one that encouraged convicts to express their inner selves
and finer feelings. Old habits dying hard, Boyle grabbed the chance
with both hands. He became the Special Unit's greatest success, its
star pupil. Following his release in 1982, and truly with the zeal of

the convert, Boyle turned himself into an artistic mini-industry, penning memoirs that became movies, chancing his arm as a playwright, a wine connoisseur and, most famously, as a well-remunerated sculptor. In 1999 Boyle made his debut as novelist, with *Hero of the Underworld*, in which a newly released convict takes a stand against his former trade.

To promote this effort Boyle, as commercial custom dictates, embarked upon a signing tour. One evening in February 1999 he was due to make one such appearance, at Ottakar's bookshop in East Kilbride. The event did not come to pass. In that modern and antiseptic shopping mall, something old and vengeful was summoned, something which flew in the face of modern relativism and how it has allowed confirmed scumballs like Boyle to prosper as media celebrities.

The people of East Kilbride objected vociferously, or a certain constituency of them did: those of them of an age to have seen Gerry and the Pacemakers in concert; to have bought their bum-freezer jackets and evening gowns with wages earned in their Saturday jobs. Now in their dotage they complained in considerable number and with commendable fury. The complainants may have been getting on in years but they were capable of kicking up an unholy fuss, one which might have drawn much unwelcome attention to the retailer and its position on psychotic violence. The event was cancelled. 'Some people got quite nasty,' said the shop's manager, one Eleanor Logan. 'It was mainly older women. They remembered the bad old days.'

It was gratifying someone did. What these citizens displayed was not mere priggishness, nor the kind of disobliging paranoia that flinches at the thought of halfway houses or hostels. This was personal. The objectors would have been precisely of the age and background to have witnessed Boyle up close, back when he was red in tooth and claw. They were not persuaded to the view that his rehabilitation merited celebration. These were people with a particular and a pain-filled relationship to Boyle. For them, his name brought to mind not the impressive attention to period detail shown in the latest cinematic telling of his story. His name did not evoke the rights and wrongs of prison reform. They thought first not of Boyle's sculptures – lumpy things, usually depicting men in pain – nor of his impressive *riad* in Morocco; nor of his marriages to sundry well-meaning sympathisers or his work with young offenders. They hated Boyle not for what he had – money, fame, social standing – but for what he lacked: humility, tact, the decency to shut up and go away. What came to their minds was the cold fear and superstitious dread felt by families, friends and acquaintances on hearing Boyle's knock on the front door. They thought of hard-working men flailing in their sitting-rooms, blood in their eyes and scimitar scars across their faces, for having broached one of Boyle's arcane codes of honour. They thought of the disgrace and embarrassment Boyle had for four decades cast over their city. They had had their fill of Jimmy Boyle first time round and were damned if they'd pay £10 to read about it now.

And bloody good for them. Would that other cities refused so firmly to indulge their celebrity miscreants; we might have been spared 'Mad' Frankie Fraser, Dave Courtney, John McVicar, Charles Bronson, Freddie Foreman, Chris Lambrianou and all the other superannuated maniacs now so keen to tell us how they plan to benefit society. For this is perhaps the component of Boyle's malignancy that lingers most stubbornly. He was the test case, the guinea pig, deployed to uphold the liberal argument that criminals aren't born bad but are made so by disadvantage. For certain categories of persons, celebrity criminals are very useful: to muddle-headed thespians, what we might term the Vanessa

Redgrave-class, itching to display the generosity of their empathy; to prison reformers, with their hobby horses; to any number of single-issue rabble-rousers and system-smashers; to editors and publishers, bent on soaraway sensationalism; to malcontents claiming that famous criminals are kinds of folk heroes. Since the publication in 1977 of his memoir *A Sense of Freedom,* Boyle has been the megaphone through which those so-minded have disseminated their conspicuous forgiveness. Many artisans have form in this respect. In the 1980s Norman Mailer advocated the authorial talent of prisoner Jack Henry Abbot, to the point where Abbot's memoirs *In the Belly of the Beast* were published to rave reviews, soon after which Abbot was charged with killing a waiter in New York. More recently, showbiz elites have been dogged in their support of the film director Roman Polanski, who is threatened persistently with extradition to America on charges of sexual assault. Once he had relocated to Edinburgh, Boyle became a coveted guest at the dinner tables of the city's upper middle-class, flaunted like an exotic pet.

This is all some distance, admittedly, from a gang of uppity pensioners in an East Kilbride bookshop. It isn't quite, though. The soft-headed, the impressionable, the gullible and the pious have long maintained that a certain kind of experience is privileged: the experience of the outsider, the outlaw, the criminal, driven to aberrance by disadvantage, sacrificed on society's altar in order that the rest of us can live in peace and prosperity. Few figures have served more effectively as the focus of this tendency than Jimmy Boyle.

Dan Brown

Dan Brown is an author, as will be known to anyone who purchased his novel *The Da Vinci Code*, most probably in an airport terminal, or stacked alongside eight further copies in a charity shop. He is a tremendously successful author, yet also a tremendously poor one. Since publication in 2003, *The Da Vinci Code* has simultaneously enjoyed the bliss of the elect and the tortures of the damned. Brown's success is envied by every author on earth. The novel has sold more than eighty million copies, been translated into forty-four languages and adapted to become a cinema blockbuster starring Tom Hanks. By all standards, it has been a global phenomenon. Yet also it was derided universally; partly for its theme – intrepid investigator defies an ecclesiastic conspiracy to uncover the secret marriage of Jesus Christ – but principally for its prose, which read as though Brown typed it while wearing boxing gloves. It was a book which brought to mind Dorothy Parker critique that 'this is not a novel to be tossed aside lightly but thrown with great force'. Certainly, the book provoked questions – who were the Knights Templar? Where is the final resting place of the Ark of the Covenant? And why does every copy of *The Da Vinci Code* have the corner of page forty-six turned down? This last conundrum is answered easily: page forty-six is as far as any sensible person can read without starting to gnaw at their wrists. To solve these mysteries required bold, lateral-thinking individuals. In their absence, illiterate mouth-breathers had to suffice.

Let us pick a passage from the novel at random. This is from page thirty-six of the British edition: 'The captain arched his eyebrows."Your French is better than you admit, Monsieur Langdon". My French stinks, Langdon thought, but my zodiac iconography is pretty good.' Thrilling, isn't it? As you can tell, characters speak in a weird, explicatory fashion intended to benefit those who read with their index finger. 'Ah, professor,' you half-expect to hear; 'We haven't met since the conference on Egyptian symbology when I shocked the academic establishment by revealing the archeological substructure of King Solomon's temple, after which my wife Deandra, a former underwear model, divorced me and gained custody of our seven-year-old daughter Kimberly, who is dyslexic.'

The novel's utter want of felicity, however, did not deter legions researching for themselves its sundry conspiracies, most famously those relating to Rosslyn Chapel, a kooky little God-shop in the countryside near Edinburgh. Regarding Rosslyn, even to the heathen the chapel is a remarkable thing; sublimely strange and beautiful. It was built in the mid-15th century as a private chapel for the Sinclair family, and decorated internally with all manner of carvings. Patterns and symbols proliferated; Green Men were all around, foliage growing from their mouths. More than two hundred small stone boxes dotted the walls, their significance still uncertain. The chapel is a symphony in sandstone, enhanced to the extreme with fanciful elaboration. Over the centuries, theories grew to explain the intentions behind it. Some thought the carvings hinted at Masonic links, or an association with the Knights Templar, a shady chivalric order dating back to the Crusades. Nobody knew for certain; speculation flourished wildly. So Rosslyn had long been an enigma, a tantalising anomaly known mainly to liturgical and architectural historians.

And then came Dan Brown, and with him the waddling and the credulous of five continents. *The Da Vinci Code* made several striking postulations, principally that Rosslyn Chapel is central to the question of Christ's bloodline. The Holy Grail, suggests the novel, was interred beneath Rosslyn, a result of the illustrious connections of the Sinclair family, and was either the remains of Mary Magdalene or a set of papers confirming the union between her and Christ. This truth was referenced by the chapel's decorative effulgence. The distinction of its purpose was alluded to by the singularity of its design. Brown wasn't the first to make claims around the domestic arrangements of the Saviour. They had existed for centuries in regional traditions and were summarised in *The Holy Blood and the Holy Grail*, a speculative examination of the legends published in 1982. Brown bolted such mysticism to an action-adventure plot in which a police cryptographer finds herself at the centre of a series of murders. The writer threw in a miscellany of esoteric bric-a-brac: numerology, symbology, cryptography, Vatican conspiracy, assassin monks and more. Not that Brown was happy to concede as much, insisting in interview after interview that '99 per cent' of the book was true. Certainly 99 per cent was badly-written, as evinced here: 'Captain Bezu Fache carried himself like an angry ox. His dark hair was slicked back with oil, accentuating an arrow-like widow's peak that divided his jutting brow and preceded him like the prow of a battleship. As he advanced, his dark eyes seemed to scorch the earth before him, radiating a fiery clarity that forecast his reputation for unblinking severity in all matters.'

God knows how but the cocktail caught fire. Brown became a phenomenon and Rosslyn Chapel a must-see for every impressionable, spookily-minded tourist visiting the British Isles. Which is where the difficulties really began. For half a millennium Rosslyn had lain undisturbed, mute and mysterious in the Midlothian rain. Suddenly it resembled an airport gift shop, beset by every wearer of breathable rainwear in the first world, as the dim of every nation descended. Access became so difficult that entry became by official tour only. Academics lined up to pick apart Brown's hypothesis, issuing rebuttals that deflated the occult bubble. The chapel's floor plans, they countered, revealed Rosslyn was modelled not on King Solomon's Temple, as claimed, but on Glasgow Cathedral. X-ray investigation failed to locate the Holy Grail. Brown was shown repeatedly to have played fast and loose with liturgical history. He was shown to be in a long tradition of fabulists, hoaxers, bluffers and sensationalists. Yet few minds were changed. Rosslyn Chapel was by now firmly on the gazetteer of inter-continental irrationalism, alongside Area 51, Loch Ness and the Nazca desert. Like a button-down Merlin, Brown had transmuted several pages from his ur-text, *The Holy Blood and the Holy Grail*, a widely discredited slab of fanciful dross, into commercial gold.

It was Rosslyn Chapel that bore the brunt. Change was swift, even more so once the book had become a movie and yet further constituencies were exposed to its arrant gibberish. For centuries this enchanting and sacred site had slumbered. Now, as happened with the monoliths of Stonehenge, trustees were obliged to take steps. A vaunting steel canopy was erected over the chapel, compromising its beauty considerably. The upsurge in visitor numbers, from 40,000 a year to 175,000, meant more fingers eroding the ancient stone, more feet pounding the naves and transepts. Further nutters crept out of the woodwork, like Dr David Conley of Oregon, who lobbied trustees to allow him to scan the chapel electronically. Perhaps fearing his electronic apparatus consisted of a *Star Trek* phaser and a metal detector from Argos, the trustees refused. Conley then discovered that he happened to be a direct descendant of a Knights Templar grand master. This was the kind of marzipan Rosslyn had to deal with, and deals with to this day. 'There is a danger that so many people brushing against the sandstone features could have a damaging effect,' said the chapel's project manager Stuart Beattie. Or is he? It won't have escaped your notice, surely, that Stuart Beattie is an anagram of Denier of the Truth, if you use an ancient Hebraic alphabet and add the letters D, R, T and H. Was this a coincidence? Surely not. Two millennia of cover-up is one thing, but it is nothing against the curiosity of Elmer from Delaware and his charming wife Carole. This curiosity bedevils Rosslyn Chapel still, turning a jewel of Scotland into a hotspot of bunkum, and all thanks to the mystic hyperbole of Dan Brown.

Robert Burns

In 1790, the English radical and mystic William Blake published 'The Marriage Between Heaven and Hell', a verse meditation on Biblical themes, and a poem of profound and awful majesty. That year also, Robert Burns, later crowned Scotland's Bard of Immortal Memory, wrote 'Tam o' Shanter', in which a drunk watches on as the devil plays bagpipes in a church. No single comparison says more about the Scottish soul, and its core of couthy, sentimental banality. In pursuit of same we fast forward to 1834, when the then-unmarked grave of Burns was prised open and inspected; such seemed to pass for entertainment in 19th century Dumfriesshire. It was a grave which Burns did well to avoid for so long, even though he died at thirty-seven. He was physically decrepit, with Kussmaul's disease, systemic lupus erythematosus, carcinomatosis and heptatitis among the likely causes. He was sexually incontinent and financially irresponsible; a man who, as one critic put it, failed to reach 'moral manhood'.

At this time the pseudo-science of phrenology, the study of character as expressed by cranial indentations, was at its height, or depth, and Burns, clearly, was a phrenological prize to die for. The skull was analysed by one George Combe, who was kept ignorant of its owner's fame. Combe concluded that, in life, the subject had possessed high levels of 'combativeness', not to

mention 'philoprogenitiveness', which was late-Hanoverian slang for the inability to keep it in one's trousers – a shrewd summation, given that Burns sired numerous illegitimate offspring. Less definitive, though, was Combe's verdict on what the head told us about Burns' linguistic abilities. The best the lump-inspector would hazard was 'uncertain'.

And don't we know it. Among the more bizarre aspects of life in Scotland is the veneration of a poet whom few are able to decipher, who penned what to the modern ear is indistinguishable from gibberish. Burns wrote in standard English sometimes but more often in lowland Scots, the argot of farm labourers and ferret baiters. To wit, this extract from one of Burns' most famed works, 'To A Mouse': 'Wee, sleekit, cow'rin, tim'rous beastie/O, what a panic's in thy breastie!/Thou need na start awa sae hasty/Wi' bickering brattle!/I wad be laith to rin an' chase thee/Wi' murd'ring prattle!' Actually, that one's relatively clear. Try this, from the afore-mentioned 'Tam o' Shanter': 'O Tam! had'st thou but been sae wise/As ta'en thy ain wife Kate's advice!/She tauld thee weel thou was a skellum/A blethering, blustering, drunken blellum.' Now, without wishing to come over like a Romford brickie, little of the previous makes much sense and, anyway, as poetry, once the rustic chaff has been hosed off, it is scarcely surpassing. At best, then, we might consider Burns a colourful footnote, a rural prodigy, albeit one whose literary merit is, to say the least, questionable.

In modern Scotland, however, such opinions are heresy. Burns is forever a hero, an Achilles, Scotland's leading man. He is worshipped for his poetry and also for his politics, being of a mildly radical, leftish hue wholly in keeping with the revolutionary tenor of his times. Schoolchildren are obliged to commit his verse to memory, as if it were the teachings of Chairman Mao. His birthday is celebrated lavishly, with Burns suppers where the main course, always haggis, is addressed as if it had the ability to reply. Unfailingly, senior politicians quote Burns when stuck for the wise yet waggish *mot juste*. No large public event or celebration is allowed to pass without some dignitary struggling to their feet and reciting a Burnsian mouthful of spittle-spraying plosives. The Scottish parliament was opened in 1999 to the strains of a woman singing 'A Man's A Man For A' That'. Legislation paving the way for the independence referendum was introduced on 25 January, Burns' birthday. We have only to read Andrew O'Hagan's introduction to the 2008 edition of Burns' work – with its depiction of the poet travelling to Edinburgh on a donkey's back – to appreciate the messianic, Christ-like terms in which the Scots have cast Burns. Regard for the man has assumed an almost religious fervour. Any sceptics, meanwhile, see only a plaster saint at the head of a charismatic cult.

When you witness the response to Burns apostasy you understand why there is so little of it. In 2008, the broadcaster Jeremy Paxman wrote a foreword to the newest edition of the Chambers Dictionary. He had a go at the poet. It was as though he'd punched a stranger's horse outside an Alloway tavern. Burns, he conceded, did have his uses, though mainly as a source of interesting lost terms, such as *forswunk* (meaning tired) and *ramfeezled* (meaning tired also – Burns liked to put himself about). Otherwise, said Paxman, the poet was merely 'a king of sentimental doggerel'. The fellowship closed ranks: 'What Paxman said is obviously not true at all, it's just that English folk today don't read Burns any more,' said novelist Alasdair Gray. 'This is the ridiculously Anglicised view of someone who completely misunderstands the deep satire of Robert Burns,' added a professor of Scottish literature. Pointedly, Alex Salmond, for there's no show without Punch, quoted 'To A Louse': 'O wad

some pow'r the giftie gie us, to see oursels as others see us.'
Whether anyone understood him, though, is another matter.

The definitive biography of Burns, *Dirt and Deity*, was written by
one Ian McIntyre, a former controller of Radio Three. He added to
the book a chapter analysing this rise in Burns cultism then fell foul
of it himself. This was in 1996 when he proposed comparing Burns'
DNA against that of an infant interred in a Greenock cemetery,
possibly yet another of the poet's illegitimate offspring. The Burns
community, demonstrating as much enthusiasm for the plan as the
cardinals of Turin show for scientific testing of their famous shroud,
denied McIntyre access to the necessary locks of the poet's hair.
Clearly the less savoury side of Burns was deemed to need no further
light shone upon it. And so the beatification continues.

Clearly, the project is nationalist in origin; its most hagiog-
raphic phase has been wholly post-devolutionary. One can see why
Burns is useful to them. He's been good for a few catchphrases, the
ones involving auld acquaintance, men being men for a'that and
the superlative tastiness of haggis: 'Fair fa' your honest, sonsie
face/Great chieftain o' the pudding-race!' Unlike, say, Lord Byron
he died too young to do anything properly shaming. Time ran out;
prior to his death Burns had been planning to run slaves into the
Americas. He was good-looking and personable and, most impor-
tantly, he had no involvement whatsoever with England. He
embodied Scotland's conceit of itself, of opposing social inequity
while getting the drinks in. If Burns hadn't existed modern
Scotland would have invented him. It'd had a practise run at this,
of course, with the Ossian poems, a heap of mythic hokum that
appeared, coincidentally, the year after Burns' birth. It is pretty
golden, until we consider the foundry of Burns's fame, his poetry.
And then we appreciate what a manure-splattered lightweight the
Bard of Immortal Memory truly was.

John Calvin

I t's a long way from the door of a church in medieval Germany to a set of childrens' swings in a municipal park on the Hebridean island of Lewis. But such are the extremities we associate with John Calvin, religious reformer and holy father of the Free Church of Scotland, one of the most derided institutions the place has yet produced.

It was in 1517 that Calvin, a Catholic priest, nailed to the church in Wittenberg his Ninety-Five Theses. At the time the Catholic church was attempting to raise money by flogging to the faithful what it termed indulgences: instant absolutions and pardons from sin; in effect, spiritual get-out-of-jail-free cards. The Ninety-Five Theses were Calvin's list of objections to the practice. Forgiveness, he argued, was granted by God alone rather than by some sanctified accountant in Rome. Such false assurances, he added, could only serve to weaken true faith. 'As soon as the coin in the coffer rings,' Calvin satirically quoted, 'the soul from purgatory springs.' Thesis 86 expressed the nub of the matter: 'Why does the pope, whose wealth today is greater than the wealth of the richest Crassus, build the basilica of St. Peter with the money of poor believers rather than with his own money?'

For Calvin the theses were academic arguments rather than broadsides. He was attempting to stimulate debate rather than

step on toes. But such was not how his work was taken. Gutenberg's printing press was the latest thing and the theses were seized upon. Soon, his text had travelled to Italy, France and England. Calvin became something of a theological celebrity. Students packed out his appearances. The faithful demanded more of his super, soaraway meditations and Calvin obliged, with such page-turners as *On the Babylonian Captivity of the Church* and *To The Christian Nobility of the German Nation*.

To gratify his public Calvin hit the road, lecturing wherever he was wanted. It was during this period he realised that, yes, actually, he did have issues with Vatican dogma, now you came to ask. Most particularly with the Catholic idea that believers work in cooperation with God, that their faith is nurtured jointly, deity and believer working in conjunction. To Calvin this seemed rather cheeky. The righteousness of God, he argued, came wholly from outside the believer, was placed into him. All, he wrote, are justified without their own works and merits, by God's grace alone. Salvation, therefore, was a matter of predestination, of having been chosen by God to be his spiritual receptacle. And if you hadn't been, tough luck.

The doctrine of Calvinism later appeared in a gentler form, Lutheranism, but its purest variety had taken root in Scotland, as the nation strove to reduce the influence exerted by Catholic France, embodied in Mary, Queen of Scots. The doctrine, though, had taken root best in soil of a stridently particular sort, that of the Western Isles. Elsewhere in Scotland, Calvinism would be softened over time by the need for a more adaptable, consensual kind of faith. Hidden from scrutiny and absolved of accountability, however, the islands incubated Calvinism in its purest form, with all its attendant antipathy to Rome's seductive trappings. Here, faith was to be plain and unadorned, reliant heavily upon Biblical recitation and requiring from its adherents a quite conspicuous form of abjection. There was to be no colour, no enjoyment, no sense that believers were engaged in any kind of relationship with God, who, anyway, was demanding and wrathful. The game had but one name: pray hard and hope for the best.

Over four centuries, then, the Calvinists, as gathered into the Free Church of Scotland, have come to be seen as like something from the pages of *National Geographic*, a tribe of the defiantly odd, like the Amish in North America. As a nation, we mock gently their demeanour; the men in their overcoats and Homburgs of Bible-black, their unsmiling faces carved from granite and radiating a pious fearfulness, as they walk slowly to their grey and cheerless churches. The Calvinists, or as they're known colloquially the Wee Frees, are like some weird growth, separate but attached, and committed utterly to a long-vanished principle few of their countryfolk know of or care about. Which, of course, is their prerogative. Generally, most Scots are too tickled to be truly bothered by the Wee Frees. As long as they stay hidden within the nation's skirting-board they can worship goats should they care, and may well do, for all the rest of us know.

There is an exception here, however: the strict Sabbatarianism of the Wee Frees. Now, this was just a nuisance. On Sundays, the islands – Lewis, Harris and the Uists particularly – became *verboten* zones; no ferries, no flights, no buses. Some remain so. And each time the spectre of seven-day operation appears we have the sight of men in Homburg hats picketing ferry terminals and throwing themselves like suffragettes into the paths of container lorries. In the mid-1990s, after the landing of Sunday newspapers was partially restricted, there was discussion on Lewis, I recall, as to whether similar success could be achieved on Sundays with regard to the island's internet signal. It remains one of the great cautionary tales of Scottish life that the childrens' play parks on Lewis would be deactivated on Sundays, by the tying together of the chains of the swings. The truth of this, only God knows. If nothing else, this is the place to ask Him.

Billy Connolly

The Scotia Bar has changed little in the past four decades, though this isn't so true for the area surrounding it. Stockwell Street, running south from the city centre to the River Clyde, has had its face washed and its teeth capped. Now, the tenements sit close by business hotels built from beige brick, or they've been swept away completely to create cheerless acreages of car parking. But the bar itself persists, still a close-packed little place, with oak-panelled walls and a rough clientele with faces like melted candles. There is only one trace of the bar's best known customer; a curling snapshot stuck – with an eye for the allegorical, perhaps – right next to the cash register.

The Scotia has long been considered the foundry of Billy Connolly's career, the place where he learned to transmute the growling banter of howff and shipyard into a style that would conquer the show business world. This it duly did. Today, Connolly is perhaps the most famous Scotsman on earth, a status he acquired by sheer force of personality. Obviously his comedy contributed vastly, with its winningly aggressive insights into male bemusement. But the comedy was inextricable from the character. We think not so much of Connolly's routines as of his bearing, his presence. He peddles more than mere entertainment. He was the megaphone through which the industrial working class of Scotland proclaimed

its existence. The work and the man are of a piece, harmonised in that compelling blare of a voice, engraved into caricature as an explosion of wiry hair, made unforgettable by his close resemblance to a force of nature. Connolly is not so much an entertainer as a sermoniser, a comic Rasputin.

And this, as he has demonstrated, is not an easy thing to be. It is difficult to credit that this once-brilliant entertainer became such a copper-bottomed twerp – a twerp not because he got rich, successful and privileged; but because he has ended up precisely the kind of character he once lampooned: a bumptious bully, a pompous boobie, a self-adoring chancer, a figure who can brook no opposition. Connolly's flaws have revealed themselves with the passing decades, to the point where he now borders on the unbearable. He keeps up that 1970s showbiz habit of attacking reporters, on grounds a six-year-old child could show to be poorly argued. He endorses the howling marzipan of his psychotherapist wife Pamela Stephenson. He does this even while refusing to recognise his own psychopathology, that of a brittle weakling compelled to clamp his hands over his ears at the first syllable of criticism. He comports with royals and plays the laird on his Highland estate because not to do so, he has argued, would be elitist. He pours his remaining talent down the drain half-a-pint at a time with back-slapping travel documentaries. His insistence on behaving like a teenager into his senescence speaks of profound psychological trauma. He pulls off the trick of being simultaneously impressionable and dictatorial.

Even at his height, and even for all his popularity, Connolly was always an acquired taste. As his first biographer Jonathan Margolis put it in *The Big Yin: The Life and Times of Billy Connolly*: 'He provokes a peculiar reaction in Scotland, in America, Canada, New Zealand and Australia. Young people think he is a has-been, the middle-aged that he is a never-was. The elderly think he is too filthy; alternative comedy fans that he is too clean; while hippies insist he is a sell-out.' As soon as he appeared in the early 1970s common wisdom quickly had it that Connolly lacked comic invention and had merely polished up for public consumption what he'd heard on street corners. In the process he depicted his own people as scowling, unlettered drunks. But that argument was put to one side when Connolly found himself feted by the light entertainment establishment in London, though this was to create difficulties of its own. From being considered too close to his roots Connolly was then judged too distant, certainly as the 1980s progressed and he underwent the personality boil wash that saw him emerge as a vegetarian Buddhist teetotaller in a linen suit, performing material about Reiki healing and baby alarms.

On many occasions Connolly gave a personal audience to Michael Parkinson, an old friend and a toothless acolyte. His authorised biographies were written by his wife, *Billy* and *Bravemouth*, books with all the objective rigour of a Valentine's card: at one point Stephenson even describes the infant Connolly as a 'future enemy of the bourgeoisie'.

Airports became the sole chink in his armour, the one place the hornet of the press could corner him. It was in an airport, Heathrow, in 2004, that Connolly was called to account for one of the most regrettable episodes of his career. On stage at the Hammersmith Apollo the week previously Connolly had discussed the plight of Ken Bigley, an English engineer taken hostage in Baghdad, commenting on the man's young Thai wife and saying of his threatened execution: 'Don't you wish they [the abductors] would just get on with it?' Connolly claimed he'd been quoted out of context. Few believed it and the row rumbled on until the moment Connolly was departing for his (then) home in Los

The Edinburgh Bookshop
219 Bruntsfield Place
Edinburgh, EH10 4DG
Telephone 0131 447 1917
E-mail mail@edinburghbookshop.com
VAT 150 5493 22

Blood Guard Bk 1 The Blood Gua   £7.99
Summoner Bk 1 The Novice   £7.38
Gone   £7.99
Nemesis   £7.99
50 People Who Screwed Up Scotl   £8.99

Number of Items: 5

Subtotal.   £40.95

Total.   £40.95

Payment

Card: £40.95

Visit us on www.edinburghbookshop.com

------ VAT SUMMARY ------

Vat @ 20%.   £0.00

Date   28-Jun-2018 13:17:35
Receipt 92,241

Angeles. 'I've got nothing to say. Why the fuck would I want to talk to you? I don't give a fuck if you are asking me a question. I don't know who you are. You're the enemy.' Pressed on whether he was sorry for the joke, he added: 'Never mind. I don't want to talk to you. You're a prick. Go and hassle Elton.'

And, so, we find Connolly deep in his imperial period. Nowadays, comedically, he is merely a lightning rod for whichever random notion happens to strike him. He is the verbal diarist of a life whose substance is determined by its own celebrity. He tells us the difficult truth of how it feels to bump into Jack Nicholson twice in the same afternoon. It is no easy task to find the Connolly of forty years ago – folksy and demotic – within the portentuous and fatiguingly splenetic performer of today. The contemporary Connolly show is one long digression on how it feels to be Billy Connolly. The audience is pulled along by that Partick foghorn of a voice and by the mesmerising force of the performer's self-fascination. These days Connolly performs not comedy but a kind of spoken autobiography. Yet the only truly funny thing about him is the degree of seriousness with which he seems to take himself.

Sir Sean Connery

Actors and knighthoods: a tricky conjunction. Does donning the motley ever merit bestowal of the highest honour in the land? Maybe at one time it did, in recognition of an actor's longevity and dedication to their craft. Most of us grew up hearing so frequently the name Sir Laurence Olivier we came to suppose the Sir component was simply something Larry had been christened with.

Likewise Sir Ralph Richardson, Sir John Gielgud or Sir Donald Wolfit. Something about the Sir bit suggested the recipient had made their bones as nobly as their profession allowed, on stages lit by gas lamps, amongst colleagues who'd known Shakespeare personally. It was an appellation redolent of actor-managers, of Command Performances, of school parties staring glumly at matinee productions of Sheridan. You heard the Sir and pictured thespians bravely giving us their Bottoms as all around the Luftwaffe dropped its bombs.

All changed now, of course. These days, knighthoods are doled out like *TV Quick* awards. We think, for instance, of an uppity squit like Ben Kingsley, lambasted widely for insisting, against all tradition, that his title be used on his film posters. Or we look over the roll-call of past recipients, note the name Charles Hawtrey and think, God, surely they didn't give one to the *Carry On* actor? You

wouldn't put it past them. But, no, actually the honour was for a namesake, a Victorian stage director.

And what of Sir Sean Connery, so-called Greatest Living Scot? He is trickier yet. With the best will in the world, even with in-depth knowledge of the seven James Bond films in which he starred, it is properly difficult to understand why Connery was so commended to distinction. We enumerate the possibilities. Was it because that as an actor Connery was technically unmatched, a virtuoso of diction, projection and expression? Don't be ridiculous. Few thesps have made so little go so far or found themselves so parodied for their wholesale inability to render on screen anything but a lightly modified version of their own self.

Medieval Italian monks, futuristic bandits, Edwardian archeologists, Robin Hood – Connery has played them all and found within each some hitherto unsuspected traces of an Edinburgh background. Perhaps the knighthood recognised Connery's tireless work for good causes, as a UNESCO ambassadorship did for Sir Roger Moore? Dream on. Connery did, admittedly, donate to charity his fee from the 1971 James Bond film *Diamonds Are Forever* but, otherwise, he is not especially known for his contributions to charity. Maybe Connery was knighted for incarnating a breadth of well-loved characters. This was true for Sir Michael Caine who brought to life Alfie Elkins, in *Alfie*, Harry Palmer, in *The Ipcress File*, Jack Carter, in *Get Carter*, and a panoply of others. With Connery, though, reasoning of this sort runs quickly into difficulty. Excluding the James Bond films, can anyone name more than, say, three movies in which Connery appeared? Probably not. He preferred to fill his time with well-remunerated, straight-to-Betamax fare, with shlockbusters such as *Meteor*, *Entrapment* and *The Rock*. By any standard Connery's career was a gout of pulp, one hunk of cinematic carbohydrate after another. Much of it we blush to recall: *The Wind and the Lion*? *Zardoz*? *The First Great Train Robbery*? *Cuba*? Mockery of this type would mean naught to the man, though. On Connery, the words *quirky* or *low-budget* acted like sunlight on Dracula. He seldom found anything noble, creative or challenging in his profession. Rather, he was a male model born beneath a four-leaf clover, a slab of bodybuilding beefcake described by Bond creator Ian Fleming, disgruntled by Connery's casting, as 'an overgrown stunt man', a hack upon whom fortune smiled. His shortcomings in competence and professional reputation have never been the sticks and stones with which to break his bones.

This, however, did not prevent Connery becoming horridly thin-skinned. As the world's media were to discover in the wake of the Bond phenomenon, few stars could harbour such a want of grace or gratitude. Compared against Connery, teething toddlers were paragons of civility. It wasn't that the actor was actively hostile or combative like, for instance, Billy Connolly, so much as sullen and disobliging, a glowering tower of disgruntlement. There was to Connery something as forbidding and unapproachable as the crags looming over his native Edinburgh. Neither did he seem of a piece with colleagues and peers. He had little of the larky levity of Caine or Moore, none of the theatrical gravitas found in Tom Courtenay or Albert Finney, or the vitality of a Terence Stamp. Instead, like an emeritus Bruce Willis, he banged out one lump of generic hokum after another; movies sold on the height of their concept and the agreeable frequency with which the scenery exploded, all the while his talent receding as swiftly as his hairline. Connery became an island unto himself, as remote and well-protected as the lair of Dr No. From the 1970s on, Connery was a dismaying figure, a globally-famous Scot, embodiment of perhaps the greatest British cultural hero since Sherlock Holmes, yet effectively a non-presence, a refugee, a square-jawed, toupée-wearing buffoon dedicating himself, like Scrooge McDuck, to accruing the largest pile of money he could, by means of work whose quality made all too plain the cynicism involved.

And then it got worse. In the early 1970s, Connery took to espousing support for the Scottish National Party, a somewhat quixotic choice for the actor, always the least mutual of fellows. The party had been founded in 1934 and was considered still a marginal and esoteric crew, with a pipe dream for a cause and a membership comprising the whiny and the grudge-bearing. The election to Westminster in 1967 of Winnie Ewing began modifying this, as did the *It's Scotland's Oil* campaign, after which the SNP secured seven seats in the 1974 general election. In due course, constitutional change would appear on the agenda, culminating in the devolution referendum of 1979, at which the separatists were vanquished.

If anything, though, Connery's passion for Scottish nationalism deepened. A man's political sympathies are his own prerogative, of course, but with Connery and Scottish nationalism lay a contradiction as conspicuous as the Forth Bridge: he declined to reside in Scotland. Instead, Connery pursued a tax exile odyssey round the planet's sunnier spots, from Los Angeles to Marbella and ultimately the Bahamas.

Again, Connery's place of residence was his business alone. But in becoming politically vocal he rather made himself the cure that was worse than the malady. Opponents of Scottish nationalism were gifted a massive quantity of ammunition to be used against it, which was duly, repeatedly and gleefully deployed. Thus has Connery done Scottish self-determination incalculable harm, made the cause appear like the fancy of a sentimental old fool, a dilettante, a poltroon unwilling to walk it like he talked it. For this he should be thanked, of course. For more than three decades the SNP has been in thrall to a figurehead with feet of clay. In practical terms, Connery's support has amounted to cash donations, to (literally) phoned-in pep-talks played to the faithful at party conferences and to the occasional physical appearance whenever he happened to be in the country with a film to promote. He did not appear at the party's grand independence rally in May 2012. In his place were Alan Cumming and Brian Cox, actors who paid Connery some kind of obscure tribute by refusing to live in the country for which they felt such passion, like Connery for financial reasons.

One had to wonder at the bare-faced chicanery of the approach, its reluctance to acknowledge its own inconsistencies. Like the Wizard of Oz or the naked Emperor, Connery has always been painfully susceptible to the most elementary logic: that if he loves Scotland so deeply as he claims he would make his home (or one of his homes) there, pay taxes there and thus legitimise his sundry pronouncements on the state of the nation.

Instead, like a Highland estate owner of the 1800s, Connery has chosen to be a political absentee landlord, or a king across the water. Such contradictions were scarcely smoothed when, in 2000, Connery accepted a knighthood, despite nationalist antipathy to the pomp and circumstance of the British monarchy. He bent the knee to a Queen whose authority his comrades had traditionally rejected. Once more, the hard line was shown to be harder than Connery could tolerate. The attitude was hardly one to be expected of a man who once so memorably worked on her Majesty's secret service, let alone the man some persist in insisting remains the Greatest Living Scot.

Alan Cumming

I met Alan Cumming once, in a theatre on the Strand, to profile him for a newspaper. At one point in the conversation his Blackberry buzzed. Up flashed the name of the caller – Sue Gorgeous. It would have been nice to discover Sue was, say, an auxiliary nurse from Bathgate. But given that she was calling Cumming – one of the most shiningly flamboyant artistes on earth, someone once described as 'a frolicky pansexual sex symbol for the new millennium' – the greater likelihood was that Sue was the stylist who weaves peacock feathers into Cher's hair or somesuch. The actor/singer/whatever took the call and informed Sue he was unable to talk because he was having his picture taken. By dint of statistical probability, Sue should have assumed this. Cumming is always having his picture taken – usually at film premieres or Broadway first nights or at the kind of political rallies beloved of American liberal celebrities, a fraternity Cumming took pains to infiltrate. Or because he is launching his own brand of perfume. Or receiving an OBE. Or promoting his novel. Cumming exceeds the classic formulation of VIP desperation: he would turn up for the opening of not just an envelope but the opening of the cellophane pack from which the envelope was extracted. Make no mistake, in the gymkhana of modern celebrity there can be no greater show pony than Alan Cumming.

How you feel about this and about Cumming depends, one supposes, upon the temperature of your temperament. In the contemporary parlance Cumming is a Marmite kind of performer. You either love him or you itch to be left alone with him in a custody cell. You either find him twinkly and scintillating, a crisply camp delight; or you're convinced he is in the grip of a self-love so intense it borders on the pathological. You believe either that Cumming needs suitable outlets for his many talents, or the attentions of a psychopath with a large croquet mallet. Of course, similar criticisms can be made of many actors, and comedians too; each is a nightmarish breed. But Cumming takes the flaw to new, Olympian, sky-scraping, shameless heights. You rather get the impression he's been practising his autograph since the age of eight. There is little middle ground with Cumming: in the mind's eye he is either engaged in an admirable but fatiguing round of rehearsals, benefits, committees and charity work. Or he's under-taking a photoshoot for *Photoshoot Monthly* in which he sprawls naked on a bed strewn with dollar bills, laughing maniacally, while crowds in the street below scream 'Hey, Alan, New York loves your nipples!' This writer is firmly of the second opinion. There's an argument to be made that many others are too, whether they know it or not. There's no gainsaying the fact that Cumming's career has had its triumphs. Chief amongst these were the Tony he won in 1998 for playing the MC in the New York production of *Cabaret* and, in London, an Olivier award for *Accidental Death of an Anarchist*. These were the shining peaks. Way below them, however, are the litter and detritus. Cumming has had the kind of professional life that suggests his answering machine announces: 'Hi, you've reached Alan. I'll do it.' Not even Orson Welles in the frozen-pea and sherry advertising doldrums of his career approached his day job with such wanton, cheque-pocketing promiscuity. You name it and Cumming will turn up bright and early Monday morning to chew his way through it: the role of Bruno the Bear in television series *Shoebox Zoo,* for instance; or a video-game voiceover; or cameos in the movie versions of *The Smurfs* and *Garfield*; a thousand campy walk-ons in a thousand American sit-coms; or his recurring role in the television series *Robot Chicken.* Over the remainder it would perhaps be kindest to draw a veil, or perhaps a tarpaulin. Suffice to say, it is difficult to identify another actor so hell-bent on forgetting the quality in favour of feeling the width. There are headless pigeons with a methodology clearer and more cogent than the one employed by Cumming. It is truly a grim day when we look to the acting profession for discretion and constancy but this is what Cumming obliges us wistfully to do, such is his own hog-snorting, rip-roaring stampede for an orgiastic, omnipresent kind of ubiquity. You wonder why Cumming does it, you really do. Surely he can't need the money? He could just stay at home and admire his collection of mirrors but, then, the only person he'd hear using the phrase 'I really like what you're doing there, Alan!' would be himself. He is reminiscent of the book reviewer, as depicted by George Orwell; a man who is 'pouring his immortal spirit down the drain, half a pint at a time'.

So who is Cumming anyway? As with Piers Morgan, there are two versions of him: the British one and the American one. When he'd been based in the UK Cumming had been mildly diverting, as a spear-carrier on television soap operas and in revue a campy lampooner of the Scottish *bourgeois gentilhomme*, with the Victor and Barry double act he and Forbes Masson performed through-out the 1980s. The 1990s brought a starker commitment to sexuality and its politics. Cumming split from his wife, actress Hilary Lyon, declared himself bisexual and became a poster boy for everyone on the wilder shores of the sexual mainstream, with his campaigning for sexual health and his theatrical choices: in *Bent, Cabaret* and as Dionysius in the National Theatre of Scotland's production of *The Bacchae*. It was in America, though, that Cumming realised himself fully and spun out most vigorously the kaleidoscopes of his sexual and showbiz identities. In 2008 he adopted dual citizenship.

You will have noticed that some of the remarks above are prescriptive and presumptuous. Who are any of us to criticise a man's freely made, law-abiding choices? It isn't as though Cumming brings nothing to the party more generally. He does what he can to add to the, well, to the gaiety of nations. He is by all accounts very nice to his elderly mother. He continues to work with the National Theatre of Scotland and thereby he allows a measure of Broadway star power to illuminate the stages of Glasgow and Edinburgh. He engages in the cultural life of Scotland as fully as his obligations permit, by judging theatrical awards, for example, or narrating BBC Scotland documentaries. To a heartening extent, he makes himself available and approachable. Which is nice.

By the same token, serial killers seldom get far if they refuse to leave the house. Cumming's accessibility is merely a function of his pathology, of his chronic and acute malady. This can be looked at in two ways. Cumming could behave as he does from a combination of love and altruism; because he adores performing and refuses to consider as meaningful distinctions between high and low culture, between *Phaedra* and *Garfield*. Maybe he launches perfumes and undertakes his own cable television chat shows and posts clips of his previous performances on YouTube and tweets and writes novels and journalism wholly because he nurses an abiding interest in the processes of the media, with the varying disciplines of communication. Or maybe he has found that the acclaim and adulation heaped upon award-winning actors proves in the end to be, you know, insufficient. As with all addicts, the dosage needs to be upped and the frequency of ingestion increased. No other explanation suffices. We are dealing with a man of titanic self-fascination. To an extent this can be understood: his journey from Aberfeldy to Hollywood, via *Taggart* and *Take The High Road*, has been truly impressive. Yet similar journeys have been made by many Scots: Sean Connery, Ewan McGregor and Gerard Butler among them. None appear to have the inclinations Cumming does. Who has the time, or the energy?

As a postscript to this, in January 2013 a thirty-four-year-old man from North Yorkshire appeared at Stratford magistrates court charged with two public order offences at the Olympic games the previous summer. Taken into custody the man signed his statement Alan Cumming. Meanwhile, somewhere in New York, a Scotsman turned away from his collection of antique mirrors and smiled.

Tam Cowan

Several years back BBC Scotland ran frequently a particular programme trailer. It depicted in grainy monochrome a lady pensioner struggling to climb a tenement stairwell. Beneath her breath, she lamented the freezing weather, the inadequacy of her pension, the grinding misery of penurious old age lived in a cold and damp climate. Any reasonable viewer assumed they were being alerted to a season of programmes outlining the hazards of hypothermia. The old dear made it indoors, cast off her coat and switched on her television – whereupon the room was flooded magically with sunny warmth and with views of a chubby man-child in a checked shirt he'd clearly received the previous Christmas.

Both face and shirt belonged to Tam Cowan, someone who had lately achieved near-ubiquity in Scotland thanks to his jokey treatments of indigenous football. Cowan specialised in taking what newspapers in the 1950s termed *a sideways look*. On the screen, Cowan fired another salvo of his pawky, rat-a-tat comedy, the gist of which was that each of life's little problems would be put in perspective when his latest series was seen. Consulting the statistics we find that 1,500 pensioners expired that winter, circumstances not wholly dissimilar to those depicted in the trailer. Now, this does not mean Cowan was directly and explicitly culpable for their deaths. But, then, neither does it mean that Cowan isn't a gurning, rib-nudging, mildly bizarre fellow whose prominence is to all sensible persons a matter of considerable regret.

Football is ridiculous anyway, of course, a jogging parade of unlettered, pre-orgasmic inarticulacy. Nothing of true worth or insight has ever, or could ever, be said concerning football. It is a sport famed for the mixed metaphors, non sequiturs and ball-fondling bollocks in which its practitioners speak. Drummers and footballers: widely accepted to be the two most cerebrally viscose species there are. Monty Python set the ball rolling with its footballer character who promised repeatedly he would 'open a boutique, Brian'. The cudgel was taken up by *Private Eye* and its regular Colemanballs feature: 'We watched the best of Fernando today, but he can do better' and so forth. So, clearly, there *can* be humour in football: mocking, sarcastic, satirical humour, pointing out that to take this stuff you'd need to have groin strain of the brain.

'I'm not interested in hearing someone tell a long, insightful anecdote about women's menstrual mechanisms,' Cowan has said. 'I'd rather sit down and be taken hostage by a great joke-teller. Like Stan Boardman, Bernard Manning, Jethro. It's the best feeling in the world.'

This is Cowan's level of humour, whether discussing football or matters more general. His is a rude, punning, smutty, scatological, I-say-I-say humour, very much of the kind once peddled by club comics in charity-shop tuxedos. Cowan's comedy shares a level of sophistication with the quips inside Christmas crackers, with the added drawback that you need an acquaintance with the intimate minutiae of the Scottish club game.

Let's hear one of his jokes: 'Football bosses in Birmingham are investigating a mass on-pitch brawl between two women's teams after every player on the park got involved in a punch-up. I guess that's what happens when twenty-two females turn up in the same two outfits.' Here's another: 'McCall started his career in 1982 – the same year his hairdresser retired.' Truly this is woeful stuff, barely fit to feature on an ice-lolly stick. Here's another corker: 'A ponytail on a man is the same as a ponytail on a pony. Lift it up and you'll find an asshole underneath.' A pause is left here for readers to bang their foreheads repeatedly on the nearest kerbstone. Further, Cowan's blubbery quips are marbled with misogyny. Female weight gain is harked upon constantly: 'Every time I think of Lisa Riley on *Strictly Come Dancing* my mind keeps wandering back to that clip of the elephant cub on *Blue Peter.*' Another theme is the feminine capacity for garrulity: 'In Windhagen in Germany a driver went 100 miles before realising he'd left his wife at a service station. He probably thought he'd gone deaf.' Altogether, Cowan's is an anachronistic Donald McGill, seaside-postcard world of impotent, henpecked husbands and wives who are either shrewish or overweight.

There will always, we suppose, be a market for this sort of thing, comprising manual labourers and the unskilled, the cab-driving classes, the viewers of commercial television, the sorts of people who allow their infant daughters to have their ears pierced and so on. This is fine in itself; these people are the majority, it is only proper they are represented. The issue becomes troublesome, though, when we consider who pays the bulk of Cowan's wages. It is BBC Scotland. It is not the job of the BBC to pander to the lowest common denominator, or to elevate a plainly mediocre humourist who has merely updated some very old material.

Due to some historical quirk, however, there is no BBC Scotland as such. Rather, there is BBC Lanarkshire, a mutant offshoot devoted to the needs of a million souls in the central belt. For reasons known only to itself, BBC Lanarkshire plays shamelessly to the gallery, hallucinating that its audience is several demographic rungs lower than it truly is. Hence, the station's overkill on football coverage, of monstrous sit-coms in which drunk men scream abuse at fish suppers, of misty-eyed profiles of old-time stars of Scottish variety theatre – and of populist dumplings like Tam Cowan.

Sir Arthur Conan Doyle

Doyle, of course, gave us Sherlock Holmes, possibly the most loved and enduring fictional character in the English canon, the super-rational consulting detective who through his readings of circumstance and motive penetrated deep into the soul of Victorian criminality.

Doyle (Conan was a middle name rather than part of the family name) himself was an amiable old cove, a general practitioner and bibliophile, Edinburgh-born but resident for a considerable portion of his life in Sussex. Holmes was to be his crowning achievement, though to Doyle's great dismay, a dismay inexplicable to all authors who came after. But Holmes was not to be Doyle's sole legacy. He left two: his detective – forensic, deductive, empirical – and something wholly different, something that opposed all Holmes embodied: to wit, Doyle's advocacy of spiritualism. In the twentieth century no figure endorsed and legitimised the howling nonsense of spiritualism quite like Doyle. Without him this regrettable pursuit might have stayed in the parlour and gathering hall, spinning out its conjuring tricks and sleights-of-hand, its profound dishonesties, its table-rapping, ectoplasmic duplicity.

Instead, spiritualism burgeoned exponentially. If the creator of Sherlock Holmes reckoned it, went the thinking in Edwardian England, there had to be something there, in these assertions that

the soul survives death. Doyle turned a hobby into a plague. Even yet, and quite apart from Holmes, we sense his ghost everywhere; in the newspapers, in the television schedules, in the rise of mediumship, in Spiritualism Centres and residential workshops, allied usually with the gamut of associated, but equally bogus, non-rational interests; angels, UFOs, past-life regression *et al*. Whenever some mad-haired old bag strides round an auditorium asking whether the name John means anything to those assembled Doyle is there in spirit. Whenever the recently-bereaved seek solace in some plausible fraud intermediary the shade of Doyle is taking notes. An NOP poll has found that 42 per cent of Britons believe in the empirical existence of ghosts, phantoms and apparitions; 48 per cent of Americans believe ESP is real. Nearly half of those we encounter each day, then, people with responsible jobs, with children, people left in charge of heavy machinery and fast-moving automobiles, hold opinions that fly happily in the face of all logic. Naturally, there are cultural and regional reasons behind such beliefs. But there are historical reasons too, and here the spectral figure of Sir Arthur Conan Doyle floats to the centre stage.

It is held commonly that, like so many others, Doyle turned to the supernatural in despair, unhinged by grief when his son Raymond died in the First World War. This is not wholly the case. Raised by Jesuits, Doyle was steeped in the ineffable and he deepened his interest on entering the university of Edinburgh, where he took particular note of experiments into thought transference and healing by mesmerism. After graduating, he moved south and in 1887 visited a spiritualist church in Portsmouth. He would study the subject for nearly three decades before publishing his first book on spiritualism, *The New Revelation*, in March 1918, some seven months prior to the death of Raymond (perhaps Doyle had a premonition). He adopted informally a sobriquet, St Paul of the New Dispensation. Clearly the uncanny was in the air then, a consequence of the scale of casualties, of technological change and of the cognitive jolt furnished by the growing popularity of moving pictures.

It was still pictures, however, that did for Doyle. In 1917, two teenage cousins from Cottingley in Yorkshire, Elsie Wright and Frances Griffiths, appeared in a set of photographs showing them with what they claimed were fairies living in their garden. Cursory scrutiny showed the fairies were, in fact, paper cut-outs but the claim caught fire. Weirder still, it was believed. Photographic experts at the Eastman company examined the negatives and attested they had not been tampered with. The possibility of the existence of fairies was debated widely, with the ability of teenage girls to handle a camera becoming an issue of disbelief more than the fairies themselves. And among the supporters was Doyle, who thought the pictures showed, if not fairies, then supernatural entities of some description. He invited the public to submit further evidence of the phenomenon and compiled a book, *The Coming of the Faeries*, in 1922: 'I would warn the critic not to be led away by the sophistry,' he wrote, 'that because some professional trickster, apt at the game of deception, can produce a somewhat similar effect, therefore the originals were produced in the same way.'

Doyle was embarrassed further in 1920 in an encounter with illusionist Harry Houdini. Houdini was Doyle's mirror image, a rationalist who strove to make the actual into the inexplicable. Keen to enlist him to the cause, Doyle invited Houdini to a sitting in Atlantic City, performed by his wife Jean. Houdini attended and listened politely as contact was made with his late mother. The Doyles returned to England and announced triumphantly that the great Houdini was now of their number. Hearing of the presumption, Houdini retaliated. Not only had the sitting taken place on

Houdini's mother's birthday, something she elected not to bring up, but she was able to speak not a word of English. In the decade prior to Doyle's death, his reputation never quite rallied, with this anti-spiritualist prejudice running in parallel with the controversial decision to kill off Holmes, a decision for which his readers never quite forgave him. Even yet, Doyle's indulgence of spiritualism is high on the list, runner-up to Holmes, of what we remember of Doyle. The association feeds, no doubt, on contrast, on the unlikely fact that the author behind culture's greatest rationalist espoused in private such arrant mumbo-jumbo.

In his novel *Arthur and George*, Julian Barnes takes a more forgiving line, arguing that Doyle's era was one of wonders, when all manner of impossibilities – radio, powered flight – were being mastered; perhaps establishing contact with the dead was to be considered as another such project. Perhaps. The unintended consequences, however, are around us each day, in a modern culture that takes the supernatural as a fact of life, not to mention the after-life. And all because Doyle chose to analyse the subject with the intellectual rigour not of Sherlock Holmes but of the hapless Dr. Watson.

Reginald Eastwood

The name Reginald Eastwood will mean little to you. You could, if it helps, take a moment, purse your lips, blow out your cheeks and scratch the nape of your neck thoughtfully. Yet, still, the penny will decline to drop. A distant offshoot, perhaps, of the family of the American film actor Clint? Nope. And yet you know Reginald and his works perfectly well, particularly if you have walked the streets of London.

Born in 1913, Eastwood was English and he trained as a butcher. In the late 1950s he had founded a chain of, well . . . not *restaurants* really but eating places. They were distinctive. Steak made up a fraction of their menus, that fraction being in the region of five-fourths. Diners feeling adventurous could order chips too. There was a wine list, of sorts. The walls were lined with banquettes and booths, upholstered in a strident red velvet-style fabric. These dining spaces were designed to mimic those in rough, elegant castles in the wilds of Caledonia. Eventually, there came to be hundreds of such places. They were named Aberdeen Angus Steak Houses, and they conveyed to the world a very curious take on Scotland and her native cuisine. So, let us clink our glasses of Blue Nun and say as one, Cheers, Reg.

To all intents and purposes the typical Aberdeen Angus Steak House was a mini-Scottish embassy, a theme restaurant in an era predating the invention of theme restaurants. At one time there was scarcely a street in London's West End that failed to boast (perhaps the better term is *feature)* one of these eateries on its corner. Evoking an age when Sir Bufton Tufton and chums would come down off the moors *après* some pheasant-shooting, the restaurants implied that the tables of the north were furnished by ghillies and weighed down with prime cuts of the native cow, garnished with the very same onion rings and Black Forest gateau that so nourished the boyhood of, say, Lewis Grassic Gibbon. In retrospect, it was perhaps the most ridiculed restaurant chain in culinary history.

But diners didn't visit Angus Steak Houses for the food; they went by mistake or to participate in the restaurant equivalent of *The Mousetrap*, an endless, eccentric engagement redolent of a world that vanished long ago. If a restaurant could choose its clientele you sense the steak houses would have opted for louche, MG-driving spivs in bogus old-school ties courting gullible widows. In an Angus Steak House it was forever 1964, coincidentally the year in which Eastwood sold his chain to the company behind the Golden Egg franchise, which set about the task of making Aberdeen Angus Steak Houses ubiquitous, in London at least. London was enough; representatives of every nation on earth ended up in an Aberdeen Angus Steak House, consulting their guide books with puzzled fury.

Yet, though dating from an age when rice pudding was considered a luxury beyond the reach of kings, the Angus Steak Houses survived wave after wave of culinary competition. This despite the fact that they were perpetually empty, or peopled at best by two disconsolate Japanese tourists. Like the Church of England the chain continued to be a visible presence without much visible support, setting out its altar in worship of the Holy

Trinity of rump, fillet and sirloin. You wanted to ask why the chain didn't keep up more with the times. But, then, you could have turned the question round – why should it have changed? Why bother? You were reminded of card sharks playing Find The Lady in Piccadilly Circus. Or as the comedian David Mitchell wrote in 2011: 'Not for them [the steak houses] the business model of repeat custom; their fortunes rely on the much tougher technique of trying to dupe everyone once.' There is so much passing trade in London that proprietors knew fresh meat, so to speak, would always wander in. Everyone knows that at a steakhouse you need not book. So the sad-looking tourists continued to sit in the windows, like specimens in a pet shop.

The chain's happiest days are long behind it, of course. Indeed, to write of it in the present tense is to give a hostage to fortune. It featured, famously, in an ITV documentary *Restaurants From Hell*, which revealed mouse droppings had been found in a vat of gravy at a branch in Coventry Street, W1: 'I have been doing this for seventeen years and become fairly hardened,' said the inspector, 'but even I have never found mouse droppings in the gravy – that is pretty disgusting.' This perhaps explains why the chain's corporate headquarters reacts to customer curiosity much as it might do were Chrissie Hynde and Morrissey to pop in for lunch. The twenty-seven restaurants it once ran were owned by the Turkish-Cypriot businessman Ali Salih, they served 70,000 steaks a year and had annual turnover of £30m. Now, only a handful remain; the rest went into administration in 2003. Attempting to contact corporate headquarters is difficult; even the most innocuous enquiry is met with suspicion and unreturned phone calls. It is oddly appropriate that a chain so eccentric should have someone named Sylvia Hercules as its spokesperson. I called her up. 'I'd like to speak to Sylvia Hercules please,' I said to the receptionist. 'Why?' came the response. Today, Eastwood's daughter, Lady Romsey, who married into royalty, declines to comment on what Salih has done – or not done – with her father's legacy.

Suffice to say, the steak houses, and Reginald Eastwood, did something quite unforgivable to the reputation of Scottish food around the world. Yet still it would be sad to see them vanish entirely. They are emblematic of sunnier, more innocent times; a Britain of *Carry On* films, Routemaster buses and The Beatles. To visit one is to engage in modern ritual. You half-expect the waiting staff – invariably East Europeans, with expressions suggesting how sorely they resent leaving behind beautiful downtown Gdansk – to be wearing Cuban heels. The walls are in the striking red plush that to be set off properly required the presence of Jason King or The Persuaders. Finally, you summon the will to consult the large laminated menus. It reveals you can have anything you fancy so long as it once possessed a face and was yanked mooing from its mother. Calamari, it seems, is listed as a vegetable. An unopened bottle of red wine – Blue Nun, of course – is placed on the table. This is the first rule of catering to tourists: bamboozle them with seeming kindness then, if they bite, stick it on the bill.

The banquettes create the impression you are, in a sense, inside the very thing you are eating, a circular idea that perhaps helped make the chain the leader in its field. The prawn cocktail appears to have been made from pinky seahorse foetuses and from it issues the unmistakable tang of the freezer. The diner moves on quickly, but not as quickly as the waiting staff. The main course arrives just as the last prawn has been hidden under the last leaf of lettuce. You can't help but be impressed by the iconic bluntness of the steak, the chips and the apologetic rash of salad round the outside of the plate. It is food you don't have to present, it's the Status Quo of lunch, you know exactly what you're getting; it just lolls on the plate, laughing at you for expecting something fancier. You inspect the encrusted pot of mustard and wield your knife. You sample and discover it's all a bit like eating old Enoch Powell speeches. The yeomanly lack of pretension does do something eventually, though. It suggests a forgotten age when dining out was infrequent and expensive and customers demanded to know exactly what they would be getting; when prawns were exotic, steak was reserved for celebrations and Black Forest gateau was an unimaginable extension to the vocabulary of dessert. The places feel as though they stand for a set of quaint, staid but not unattractive values. They were created for a nation intimidated by menus. Memory must not dispel wholly the timid, under-informed population for whom these restaurants were designed. And so they have a strange, faded gaiety. They display the archaeology of the last four decades of British mass dining – the institutional white coffee cups with blue rims, the place mats in racing green, the canteen napkins made of paper, the faux-decorative 'family' silver that weighs nothing at all, the sit-up-straight prep room chairs designed to induce discomfort after fifteen minutes. But the restaurants also take their place within a certain tradition. Like Balmoral or the Glorious Twelfth they're a Scottish thing that is entirely an English construct. They're as comforting, clubbable and toothlessly English as possible. In a changing world maybe it is comforting to know there are a few remaining corners of London that are forever Scottish. Even if they do always bite off more than they can chew.

Winnie Ewing

olk memory insists Winnie Ewing was the first Scottish nationalist elected to the House of Commons. She wasn't; actually, the first SNP MP was Dr Robert McIntyre, a now-obscure tailor's dummy in a thirty-piece suit who relocated his marble collection and his souvenir Scottish inventor tea-towel to Westminster in 1945 (though, lasting only three months, he was obliged to relocate them back pretty sharpish). It is telling that nationalist mythology, even of the modern kind, maintains the party's woozy relationship with empirical truth. Clearly, the Nats were not content with being wrong only about old kings and treaties with France; they itched to be wrong about the modern world too.

This is not to argue Ewing was not a figure of some consequence. For good or for ill, her arrival at Westminster was a turning point for the party. At the height of the Swinging Sixties she gave it a modern, female face. One hesitates to say Ewing gave the party glamour: hers was more of a motherly presentability than a concerted attempt to rival Marianne Faithfull. But nevertheless it signalled a departure. Pre-Ewing, the wider British mind, on the infrequent occasions it remembered to care, presumed each and every Scots Nat resembled Hugh MacDiarmid and was a small, vigorous man in tweeds and brogues, upholding the legitimacy of the Ossian poems while waging microscopic ideological vendettas

on anyone who happened to be passing. Ewing's election advanced the proposition that, while many nationalists could be like this, not *every* nationalist was. But what was Winnie Ewing like?

I met her once at her home, near Elgin. The windows were festooned with campaign stickers and posters for the party's most recent local candidate, even though the election had taken place four months previously. She showed me into the study. It was a veritable Winnie museum, a hotspot of one woman's conceit of herself as the peppery, tartan Boadicea of truth, justice and parliamentary sub-committees. On the desktops were snaps of her family: sons Terry and Fergus, the MSP for Inverness, her daughter-in-law Margaret, the MSP for Moray, and daughter Annabelle, the former MP for Perth. On the walls were framed photograph of the Queen, with Winnie's face superimposed; pictures of Winnie with Sean Connery on the parliament's opening day; and archive shots of Winnie in the guise that Britain came to know her; winner of the Hamilton seat in 1967, a primly crisp, twin-set-sporting former solicitor. Talking to her was like conversing with a Pathé newsreel. Her discourse was littered with references to Ted Heath, Harold Wilson, pit strikes, three-day weeks and with ancient, long-forgotten names such as Cunninghame Graham and Boyd-Carpenter. Whenever she commenced upon one of her many Russian-novel explanations of how some standing committee negotiated a fairer deal for fishermen in 1973 there was nothing for it but to nod, smile, settle back and set running in your mind the theme tune to *The Archers*. I wondered: did Ewing, when looking back over those decades of nationalist schism and factionalism, of internecine squabbling and nutty tub- thumping over whose pillow the tooth fairy had put the oil under, over all the repeatedly thwarted romanticism of the nationalist pipe dream, did she sometimes rest her permanent wave on the Stone of Scone,

pour herself a sherry and think to herself: well, what a waste of
time that was?

She didn't, no. Like virtually every Scottish nationalist Ewing
didn't do levity. Her life – she's eighty-four now – has been one
long hustings and awkward questions from the floor are barely
entertained. Whichever way you cut it, this was a woman whose
blood ran yellow and black. 'Has it been a waste of time?' she
mused. 'Well, we're not free so, yes, I've failed. We live in a constitutional absurdity, so, yes, I've failed. But we've established a base
camp on the climb up the mountain of freedom.'

In 1967, no one gave Ewing the ghost of a chance in Hamilton,
so her ascension to Westminster was the best works day out ever.
Footage from the time shows the carnival atmosphere when she
was paraded to the House of Commons by a flotilla of bagpipe-
squelching supporters who had travelled down by train, with
reporters treating her as part May Queen, part head of a new cult
devoted to the alien concept of Scottish home rule. Asked by one
about her ambition she replied: 'Scottish government by 1975. No
later.' It didn't work out like that, of course, but then the nationalists
have always made an art of adapting to circumstance. Devolution
was the pacifier but she was ever prepared to spit it out; her
particular strain of nationalism has always seen the promise of
devolution as a mere sop, a halfway measure, designed to dazzle
and distract.

Ewing wasn't raised a nationalist. That came at Glasgow
University, where, at the age of seventeen, she attended a lecture by
John McCormack and concluded 'that case is just unanswerable'.
Much later, her colleagues at Westminster considered it unaskable
and Ewing was ostracised, she claimed, by Labour members
angered that a safe seat had been lost to a fringe party. She did not
have a lunch table to eat at until the Liberals took pity on her. The

opprobrium forced her to put her sons in private schools, as though such bastions of the Establishment were more likely to offer a nationalist scion more protection than the local comprehensive. She described her every appearance in the House as a 'crucifixion' of insults and shout-downs, culminating, she claimed, in a series of incidents where she was stalked around the darkened palace by a Labour MP who went on to become a Lord; quite coincidentally, we assume, rather than as payback for his participation in some weird political strategy designed by Vincent Price. Another curious incident involved Ewing's son Terry and a member of the royal family. In 1974 Ewing was set to win the Moray constituency until an eleventh-hour flurry of votes from the local RAF base gave the seat to the Conservatives. On the same night, Terry was taken to hospital in Elgin by his schoolmate Prince Andrew with a suspected broken neck (confirmed later as a damaged vertebrae). Even though the incident seemed innocuous, Ewing hinted darker forces were at work, though without ever specifying what they may have been. She goes on about it yet. One hears her out and wonders if she knows what they may have been, or whether the coincidence of an election defeat, a family injury and the proximity of a royal added up in Ewing's mind to some sinister plot to impede nationalist progress. She believes this still, having declined to avail herself of the obvious remedy of asking him. Mystery, of course, is always more suggestive. Nationalists, of Ewing's vintage and currently, have always found succour in a conspiracy, whether it's the great chieftain of the genre, the misappropriation of North Sea oil, or the death of Willie MacRae, the SNP campaigner whose investigations into the Dounreay nuclear power plant allegedly resulted in his assassination in 1985.

You'd imagine by this stage in the game that Ewing, as a venerable frost-top at the apex of her own political dynasty and as someone who'd served as MP, MEP and MSP for almost forty years, would have wound up in the House of Lords. She would have loved to. But, again, fate conspired to spike her cock-a-leekie soup. Scottish nationalists have a policy: none of their number will rise to the second chamber so long as the hereditary principle remains. No, only when the House of Lords is fully elected will we see a Lord Muckle or a Baroness Spurtle. It may yet happen, by 2015. Certainly the Welsh nationalists have two Lords currently, though the Welsh nationalists also have less of a reputation for obstreperousness. Ewing was always too much a pragmatist to defy the party on the matter. But things could have been so different. If only the Nats had thought twice and undertaken the same titanic U-turn on Lords membership that it later performed on NATO involvement in any independent Scotland then Winnie could have had the ermine she so craved; though Baroness Ewing would have sounded like a character from *Dallas*.

Clearly she was not without her vanities. In 1970 she sat for David Donaldson, then Scotland's finest portraitist. In the 1990s she decided to gift the portrait to the nation. But nobody appeared to want it. Timothy Clifford at the National Galleries of Scotland could not guarantee to show it permanently; the Elgin Museum could not afford to insure it; and she was warned by George Reid that the Scottish Parliament was so haphazardly organised it might be taken down if she was no longer around to ensure its display. Instead, the Donaldson went to a humbler home, at the Glasgow Arts Club.

All political lives end in failure, said Enoch Powell, possibly ignorant of the fact that for Scottish nationalists failure is always in plentiful supply along the way too. For a generation of a certain persuasion Ewing enjoyed (but principally by her own account) an almost totemic status, as the so-called Madame Ecosse; the first resort whenever someone felt their inalienable sense of Scottishness was threatened. We will not see her like again, of such a grand, delusional slugger. We will, possibly, survive.

Donnchadh MacFhearghais

Should you find yourself on a rail platform in Scotland prepare for a curious experience. There you'll be, awaiting, say, the 10 a.m. train from Partick to Dalmarnock. Or maybe the express service from Glasgow to Tyndrum. As you idle, you will look around. Maybe you will register the dispiriting mess most Scottish railway stations have become, with their nasty turquoise fittings, murky coffee outlets and cruel aluminum seating. Casually, you will glance at the sign bearing the station's name. And then you will panic.

You are not where you thought you were. Or, rather, where you thought you were turns out to be two places simultaneously. It will seem you are travelling not from Partick but from Partaig, towards Dail Mheàrnaig. Or from Glaschu Sràid na Banrighinn to Taigh an Droma Iarach. The signs are bilingual. There is every possibility passengers may have enough difficulty speaking the language they were born with but, fear not, for here the signs are fluent in several tongues.

This second language is Gaelic, of course. And thus is engendered a curious synaptic disconnect. The surroundings are urban and cheerless, fashioned from cheap red brick and safety glass. Yet one glance at a rail sign and something other is evoked; salt spray on a Hebridean beach, the timeless peace of island life. Meanwhile, non-locals are alighting from trains in frazzled states of confusion, quizzing ticket inspectors and examining maps, as they struggle to establish if they can travel from here to Drochaid a' Chòta Meadhain (Coatbridge). The nearest Gael is more than 200 miles away, probably chuckling quietly to himself as he thinks upon the chaos and upset he has caused the lowlanders.

In Scotland the numbers who speak Gaelic are tiny; maybe 60,000, a sizable crowd at a football match. That is 1.2 per cent of the population over three years old. With an annual subsidy of £4.4m coming from the executive, disbursed by the Gaelic Development Agency, Gaelic development strategies cost us £73 per speaker per year.

Who would credit the accommodation afforded its proponents over the past two decades? Prominent in this category was Duncan Ferguson, or Donnchadh MacFhearghais to give his Sunday name, first chairman of Bòrd na Gàidhlig, or Gaelic Development Agency, the organisation within the Scottish government that is responsible for ensuring Gaelic receives all that is due to it. There is seldom a shortage of demands. If ever an entity bore out the axiom that the squeaky wheel gets the oil that entity is the Gaels. Resourceful, well-organised and persistent, the modern Gaelic lobby won't take no for an answer (it couldn't anyway – Gaelic has no words for yes or no). You name it and they want it: Gaelic schools, official status for Gaelic, a Gaelic television channel, simultaneous Gaelic translation in parliament. A so-called Gaelic Action Plan. And Gaelic signage.

Occasionally the demands are farcical but instructive. Sporadically, we witness attempts to have the provision of Gaelic road signage extended to the east coast of Scotland, where Aberdeen and Dundee are to be found. Yet in this area there is but a smattering of Gaels. You could fit them in a phone box, especially if you reversed the charges. The distribution of the Gaelic diaspora (they really do term it so) is triangular, its apex in the isles of Lewis, Harris and Skye, extending onto the mainland, its base a strip of the west coast, from Cape Wrath down to Glasgow. The diaspora hardly got as far east as Stirling, let alone Edinburgh. When economic hardship forced the Gaels to flee their islands they huddled together for warmth, principally around the economic boiler room of Glasgow.

This left a huge swathe of interior Gaelic didn't get to; or, indeed, could ever penetrate, because those areas lived with time-honoured folk dialects of their own, whether Doric in the north-east or Lallans, much further south. Happily, the bleeding obvious continues to be pointed out. Caithness Council rejected a request to erect English/Gaelic road signs on the grounds that the area contained few Gaels. Ferguson's GDA responded with warnings that public bodies would soon be obliged to observe their obligations under the 2005 Gaelic Act. Edinburgh city councillor Iain Whyte too rejected calls for a Gaelic development officer and bilingual road signs in the city: 'A council like Edinburgh is awash with strategy papers and action plans about the matters that concern its citizens and I do not think Gaelic is one of them,' he said. 'This kind of stuff comes down from the executive constantly; public servants are expected to run around like headless chickens and then, in a year's time, the action plan is gathering dust on a shelf. I'm not against the Gaelic language as such, but it's of minimal relevance to the people of Edinburgh.' The independent MSP Brian Monteith pointed out that, due to its number of law courts, more people in Edinburgh spoke Latin than Gaelic: 'There's no practical demand in the majority of Scotland for Gaelic and all Gaelic speakers can also speak English,' he said. 'The answer to the imperialism of English is not to endorse the tyranny of Gaelic in the 21st century. The Gaels have exerted on us, quite successfully, a particular type of historical blackmail.'

Clearly, then, there is no utility in or purpose to erecting Gaelic road signs in areas where there are no Gaels, just as there wouldn't be in sticking up signs in Swedish. However, utility is the least of it. The Gaels and their apologists are attempting to prove a point of principle. Gaelic, they feel, was there before all the other folk dialects. Its roots are ancient. It was the tongue in which the earliest Scots spoke, supposedly. Therefore, Gaelic is Scotland's mother tongue, and must be recognised as such, and be made to proliferate, even in places where it had no footprint. Indeed, it must be kept on life support and have the defibrillators of public subsidy applied ceaselessly to its ailing, wizened torso. The mission has to it a certain grim practicality: to replenish the numbers of Gaelic speakers at a rate that outstrips the rate at which advanced age gathers them to God.

But why? In what ways are these new speakers – mainly central belt professionals drawn to a bit of ethnic antiquity as Surrey pub landlords are drawn to horse brasses – connected with the culture that Gaelic expresses? They aren't, obviously. Gaelic is their hobby. The language becomes a code, exchanged with other central belt professionals as Klingon is exchanged between fans of *Star Trek*. And in the name of the nationalist project, where a museum of Scottish cultural mannequins has been assembled with scant regard for boring old historical fact, but with every regard given to emotional manipulation, there are plenty who are happy to help them. At an annual cost of £73 per Gael.

George Galloway

George Galloway MP begs a question. Could any public figure hold a view of themselves so profoundly at variance with that of the man on the Clapham omnibus? Surely not. The gap is chasmic. Galloway seems to see himself as nothing so much as a modern-day St Sebastian (though the Christian allusion isn't one he'd appreciate, which is precisely why I use it), assailed from all sides by arrows of cant and venality; a man of unimpeachable principle, a defender of the downtrodden, martyred for his mission of delivering inconvenient truths.

While to the rest of us Galloway is, and always will be, that swivel-eyed twit who donned a scarlet leotard and acted like a cat on *Celebrity Big Brother*. Or worse. Something about him just doesn't sit with the British public. He is too smooth, too sleekit; as oily as a teenage scalp. He steps between the raindrops, forever on the verge of reaping some vast reprimand or reckoning, yet forever talking his way out of danger. This talking is what we resent particularly, his unstemmed flow of vainglory, recrimination, accusation and geo-political pedantry. No doubt in his head it all sounds grand and righteous, like Castro at the Havana Hilton. Most detect something more akin to the quisling crowing of a Lord Haw-Haw.

On occasion, this can expose him. By way of insulting in a

debate the late polemicist Christopher Hitchins, one of Galloway's most dogged opponents, he did us the kindness of reviving the old and fragrant term *popinjay*. Naturally, he used the word incorrectly, which was only to be expected. Galloway's specialty is bombast, not finesse; a wordsmith is another thing he fancies himself to be, but isn't. A popinjay is characterised by its vanity, by an excess of regard for its own appearance. The accusation was hardly applicable to the rumpled Hitchens. Rather, it was Galloway who strove to cut what Italians call *la bella figura*. Proud at the lectern, cool in a cream colonial suit, he was voluble and restless; a wielder of the wagging finger and the table-thumping fist, stentorian and hectoring, with a pitying smirk for Hitchens ever twitching beneath his greying, sales-rep moustache. And so Galloway confronted the most renowned political commentator since Orwell as effectively as an ant confronts a juggernaut.

Like his friend and fellow exhibitionist Tommy Sheridan, Galloway helped render the Left a laughing stock. This was regrettable in Scotland particularly as the nation combated the nuisance of nationalism. Not that to Galloway this would have mattered much. Although he scrapped his way through the ranks during his early days in Dundee, Galloway found Labour an allegiance he was happy to slough off when his passions pointed him elsewhere. Throughout his (not notably successful) political career, Galloway has served his constituents as an afterthought. His true focus was Palestine and the travails of her people; a commendable cause, though perhaps less so when your employers are the electorate of dear old Blighty and struggling to meet their heating bills. Notoriously, his attendance in parliament is among the most sporadic of any sitting MP; the left-wing magazine *Tribune* once ran a classified ad reading: 'Lost: MP who answers to the name of George. Balding and has been nicknamed Gorgeous.' For close on forty years Palestine has taken priority in Galloway's mind, become the prism through which all else is viewed. He harmonised these two realities of his political life – his advocacy of Palestine and his less-than-convenient obligation to represent voters of British origin – by competing in constituencies with dispro-portionately high ethnic populations, such as Bethnal Green and Bow and Bradford West; his attempt in 2011 to become a list MSP in the Scottish parliament proved unsuccessful. Effectively he had become a single-issue politician, even if the issue in question played out beyond Britain's shores. The strategy was win-win. In the relevant areas, voters were flattered by Galloway's solicitousness and empathy and duly returned him. Little wonder he has long been known to colleagues, dismissively, as MP for the West Bank. As his career in the mainstream of British politics floundered the epithet assumed an almost literal truth.

And flounder it has. Galloway now is considered a monomaniac, a student union demagogue who gimmicked himself somehow a national platform. The transformation was accompanied by a change in presentational approach. There had been a time when Galloway was described routinely as Gorgeous George. He wasn't particularly gorgeous, not unless you were a groupie of regional savings bank deputy managers, but he did have youth and vigour. As time passed, the hair went, the skin bronzed and the wrinkles deepened, to a point where Galloway resembled a bearded raisin. When he adopted a neat little Nehru jacket garb he presented an altogether exotic sight, a world away from Westminster with its politicians dressed by their wives. Galloway was now in full pasha mode; relieved of his obligations to the Labour party, sustained by a partisan constituency, revelling in his status as the man they couldn't hang and radiating an imperious air of moral certitude. Observers lowered their expectations and Galloway didn't disappoint. There was an ongoing barney with Jemima Khan and the *New Statesman* over his marital arrangements. Separately, he expanded his brand by taking to YouTube, to panel shows and talk radio. His stunningly horrible stint on *Celebrity Big Brother* was justified on grounds that it would afford him a chance to get his 'message' across to voters, long the fig leaf of politicians seeking proximity to showbiz.

Free agent became loose cannon and a string of howlers ensued. The female population of the UK felt a shiver traverse its spine when Galloway pronounced on the matter of Julian Assange, the free speech campaigner threatened with extradition to Sweden on rape charges. Assange was accused of forcing sex upon a woman on the morning after they'd had consensual intercourse. Galloway asserted Assange had no case to answer: 'Not everybody needs to be asked prior to each insertion,' he concluded, winningly. There was the matter of the student union debate at Oxford, from which Galloway exited in high style on discovering his opponent was Israeli: 'I was misinformed,' he said, bundling his raincoat over his forearm. 'I don't debate with Israelis. I don't recognise Israel.' Sorry? Even though the discussion was to consider the proposition that 'Israel should withdraw immediately from the West Bank' and that Galloway's opponent was named Eylon Aslan-Levy?

If nothing else, this bizarre interlude occasioned a reality check. Not even Galloway could have been disingenuous enough to imagine he would not encounter Israelis while debating the actions of Israel? So, a publicity stunt, then, a means of putting the message on the front page, even if Palestine's Boycott, Divestment and Sanctions lobby were to point out that nothing in its practice prevented recognition of any given Israeli. Clearly Galloway is sunk exceeding deep in his conceit of himself as the panto villain of British politics, his every action conditioned by reaction, to an ever-proliferating cast of opponents, the spider's web with America at its centre. Oppose him and he argues you too have been infected with the virus he seeks to eradicate. Few trust, entertain or believe the man any longer. Cats, famously, even television cats, have nine lives. Galloway, surely, by now must be close to exhausting his allocation.

Ricky Gervais

Each year, the Edinburgh Festival Fringe stages without fail a particular show. This show isn't necessarily a drama, though it does bear similarities to *Who's Afraid of Virginia Woolf?*, Edward Albee's theatrical punch-up. Neither is this show humorous, not purposely. You could term it a black comedy. The show in question is the annual Edinburgh Fringe fall-out; the huff, strop or controversy that engulfs the festival city each August. We return to July 2007, when a hoarding was erected on Princes Street, close to where the Balmoral Hotel stands. It read: *Ricky Gervais Show Is Now Sold Out – What A Pointless Billboard*.

As you know, Gervais had become a star on the BBC with his sit-com *The Office*. Now he was enjoying considerable success as stage performer. He'd always been a dubious proposition, Gervais, with his vulpine gnashers, Napoleonic stature and air of half-hysteric self-congratulation. But now he was a big name and, naturally, he wished to test his mettle at the epicentre, the omphalos of stand-up comedy, the Edinburgh Festival Fringe, the mammoth jamboree to which each year flock thousands of performers, established and aspirant.

One problem, though. The show had been booked neither into a hall nor even, as befitted a performer of Gervais' popularity, Edinburgh's grandest theatre, the Playhouse. It was to take place

on the esplanade of Edinburgh Castle. By any measure, a statement was being made, and a confident one at that. The esplanade
is Scotland's driveway, a large, uncluttered space leading up to the
castle's front door. Typically, it goes unused, save for the occasional rock concert and, each year, the Edinburgh Military Tattoo,
a spectacular parade-ground tribute involving pipe bands and
marching battalions. On temporary seating 8,000 audience
members are accommodated, looking down from this vertiginous
eyrie upon the city's craggy splendour.

It was, by any definition, a good gig. But some raised their
voices against Gervais and his elevation. They believed the show
sent out the wrong signal, went against the spirit of things. Since
its inception in the 1940s, the Fringe, the largest arts festival in
the world, had been run along very particular lines. Its nature
had always been amateur, shoestring, speculative. It was a given
that in staging a show a Fringe performer would lose money,
bundles of the stuff, tossed onto the bonfire of their ambition.
Comedians, actors and transexual unicyclists alike went unde-
terred, because they prized the thrill of being amid such a
thronging cultural maelstrom.

In the 1990s this changed somewhat. What once had been
charming and shambolic, Corinthian and chaotic began to keep
its appointments and dress that bit sharper. The introduction in
1981 of the Perrier awards, the so-called Oscars of comedy, had
much to do with this. Henceforth, the Corinthian chaos was
indexed and stratified. Suddenly there was a hierarchy, a clear
prioritisation of runners and riders. And this would prove of
inexhaustible benefit to television talent scouts, flown up each year
from offices in Television Centre and the South Bank, forced for a
month to replace their rucola and sea bass with battered
carbohydrates. Though not noted as a devotee of *Puppetry of the*

Penis George Steiner, professor of comparative literature at Cambridge, expressed similar sentiments when he called for the abolition of the festival: 'They must always have the integrity to ask: should we get out while we're ahead? It takes vision and a touch of greatness to say adieu. It is the most difficult art.'

By degree, the Fringe became that most modern of entities; a shiny, sponsored, corporate bean feast, invigilated by press officers, programmers and brand managers. New networks developed. Diminished was the old model in which performers nursed dreams for which they were prepared to bankrupt themselves. To a considerable extent, the Fringe became a gymkhana where comedy management companies trotted out their charges for the benefit of commissioning editors in radio and television. With the advent of the Pleasance, the Udderbelly and the Gilded Balloon the venues too became arbiters and tastemakers. In 2012, of the 2,695 shows at the Fringe 38 per cent were stand-up. By the end of the noughties, all this was taken as a given. The amateur model was long dead. Those who looked upon the Fringe saw it for what it had become: a vast exercise in identifying, grooming and marketing new stand-up talent, ready for the lucrative pastures of the BBC Three panel show and the live DVD. And then, like a giant exclamation mark that rammed the point home, Ricky Gervais erected his billboard.

Scales fell from eyes. Hackles rose. Gervais exerted this effect at the best of times, though Edinburgh was of a different order. Few transformations in British show business had been as sudden, or as extreme, as that of Gervais. For years he had hacked along as an all-purpose jester, a smirking peddler of smutty bagatelles. After *The Office*, such was the sit-com's popularity that Gervais spent his days engaged upon a one-man ticker-tape parade. The reversal of fortune proved too swift to breed in him much humility. His ego outstripped his success. As soon as Gervais had made a name for himself he set about tarnishing it, with off-colour, weaselly-phrased quips mocking the vulnerable, yoked to a demeanour that grew pompous and boastful, as demonstrated by the horrid smugness of his Sold Out hoarding. He countered with the argument that all criticism of him was merely veiled jealousy.

In Edinburgh he could not outrun his detractors so easily. The very soul of the Fringe was being traduced, they claimed. Its history was being hijacked. One newspaper described the show as a 'comedy rally'. It was announced that tickets would be priced at £37.50, nearly four times what entry to a standard Fringe show cost. Ricky Gervais: Where Did It All Go Wrong? wondered the *Independent* newspaper. No One Finds Him As Funny As He Finds Himself, wrote the *Telegraph*. Commentators asked if the scale, spectacle and expense of Gervais' (quite literal) grand-standing would affect adversely other shows on the Fringe. Perhaps it did. What it did certainly was bring down the curtain on a particular era of the Edinburgh Fringe, an era in which this tumultuous, big-hearted free-for-all was something more than a trade fair. After Gervais, all bets were off. The contract had been torn up. Edinburgh's role as host had been usurped. Instead, the auld place became just a location, a site of necessary infrastructure, London with a castle. The transsexual unicyclists come still, but the city they inhabit is subtly changed, all thanks to Ricky Gervais and his ilk.

Mel Gibson

If nothing else, *Braveheart* gave film-goers a vision of Scotland they hadn't seen previously. A weary repertory of stock characters and scenarios had long peopled films made and set in Scotland: the dislocated prole (Peter Mullan in *My Name Is Joe*), the volatile psycho (David Hayman in *A Sense of Freedom*), the cabal of devious locals (*That Sinking Feeling, Whisky Galore!, The Wicker Man, Local Hero* – more devious locals, in fact, than you could shake a maypole at). *Braveheart* brought something fresh to the ceilidh: a conquistador, a striding Christ of a hero, ripped from the pages of history to reacquaint Scotland with her destiny. And somewhere in the misty hills of Tiree hyenas wiped from their eyes scolding tears of mirth. Two points are to be made about *Braveheart*, the directorial debut of Mel Gibson, hitherto a vigorous actor of presence and charisma. The first is that as entertainment the film – an Oscar-winning account of the exploits of medieval Highland warrior-terrorist William Wallace – is well made and thrilling. The other point is that, as history, it is remedial, beyond gibberish, radioactive bilge.

This, however, did not prevent the film becoming venerated by nationalists, in what has been one of the most pernicious Scottish phenomena of recent decades. For them, the film was catnip; wild-cat nip. *Braveheart* to Scottish nationalist was almost a kind of

pornography, a wet dream in 70 mm, damp with money shots of claymores slicing English throats, of turf sodden with ejaculations of English blood. From the cheap seats you could almost hear the groans of satisfaction as another sharpened pikestaff penetrated yet another English inner ear.

The violence in *Braveheart* was bracing in itself, but doubly so given the suspicion that, for a proportion of viewers, it was cathartic, so long as the slicing and dicing was happening to the English. Scottish nationalists take an atavistic delight in seeing the English humbled, destroyed even. Meanwhile, the neutral viewer was reminded of the sadism of the bullring or the coliseum. So *Braveheart* was a video nasty. At the touch of a remote control ancient grudges were avenged, in slow-mo were it required. You can bet it was, all the better to savour the spurting fountains of gore. Each eruption of skull-crunching mayhem was preceded by a scene in which the English generals, with their refined features and carefully-maintained facial hair, underestimated with haughty disdain Wallace and his troops. For dedicated Scots such scenes hurt like bamboo under the fingernails. Cut to several minutes later and the delicate music of broadsword meeting Home Counties kidney. 'Violence is perhaps excusable if it is violent enough,' wrote George Orwell in his survey of nationalism. *Braveheart* rather proved his point. The film is the Scottish nationalist equivalent of *Triumph of The Will*.

So much for the gladiatorial retribution, but what of the film's historical perspective? Well, would that it had offered one, beyond the evident conviction of Gibson and his screenwriter Randall Wallace that the space-time continuum can be altered at will. The SNP is never done declaring its passion for Scotland's history, yet it continues to exalt a text which recounts that history as a child might summarise a month-long camping holiday, in a garble of mistake and exaggeration. Very little of the film is in any meaningful sense true. As an example, we see the young Wallace growing up among the Highland serf class, leaping from burn to broch, ambling happily through hills and glens. In fact, Wallace was raised outside Glasgow, which even though it was less developed than it is today certainly didn't boast lochs and louring mountains. Neither was Wallace the son of humble peasants, raised by his uncle after owing his father's death at the hands of the English (rather, his father on occasion fought *for* the English). Little is known of Wallace's life pre-uprising, but documents point to his family owning estates and to his early acquaintance with soldiery. So, if not a posh boy then certainly not a straw-chewing son of the soil.

Virtually nothing in *Braveheart* held water. The film was a farrago of wish fulfillment, day-dream and masturbation fantasy. Its elevation would not be dissimilar to England nominating as its defining cinematic statement *Chitty Chitty Bang Bang*. The wilful deceptions and fantastical lies were inexhaustible. Most famously, the bulk of the movie's location work was done not in Scotland but in Ireland, which offered the filmmakers tax advantages, a policy which after six years in power the SNP has yet to adopt for Scotland. The film shows Wallace's army indicating its derision for the English by lifting their kilts in unison to expose their mocking backsides, even though the kilt was not worn in Scotland for another 300 years. Similarly, English soldiers at the time wore not smart heraldic uniforms but their own clothes. It is accepted now that Primae Noctis, the statute allowing lords to take a woman's virtue on her wedding night, used here to reveal the utter heartlessness of the imperious English, existed in fiction only. Here, the Battle of Stirling Bridge takes place not on a bridge but on rolling fields. Queen Isabelle of France – in the film Wallace's confidant and accomplice – was four at the time. Contrary to the film's romantic sub-plot, with its implication that Wallace was roused to rebellion only after the murder of his wife, he never married. The father of Robert the Bruce did not die of leprosy, nor did Robert the Bruce betray Wallace to the English. Wallace would never have worn blue face paint in battle; the practice had died out 300 years earlier with the Picts.

The scroll of mendacity runs for pages. You might counter that many historical accounts alter and exaggerate the details; that, contrary to what *Amadeus* claimed, for instance, Mozart and Salieri were on perfectly amicable terms. Films by their very nature condense, telescope and conflate. We assume it happens all the time. This, however, is not what *Braveheart* did. It invented, misdirected, concealed and perjured. Five minute's consultation of the most elementary textbook would have alerted Gibson to the errors.

He chose to overlook them. We can only speculate as to his motives. They might be best attributed to the kind of ahistorical populism demonstrated so often in Hollywood. For Scots the legend of William Wallace is one in which they might repose some degree of pride, qualified by historical knowledge. To an Australian actor working in Los Angeles, however, it was merely the tale of some guy who wears a skirt and, like, kills all the guys in the next country because the king wants to make the skirt guys, like, slaves or something.

With this as his narrative frame Gibson filled the canvas with motifs filched from *Brigadoon* and *The 39 Steps*, old westerns, sword-and-sandal flicks and afternoon television. It is to be doubted that Gibson, his big Hollywood head stuffed with visions of swimming pools, glory and lucre, saw his mission as in any way political. In his mind, he was making merely *The Wild Bunch* with bagpipes. The regrettable fact, however, is that few films have enjoyed the political after life Gibson's film has. Its timing was remarkable. This mud-caked, forest-dwelling movie blundered its way onto the dual-carriageway of Scottish self-determination, nudged along by the blithe, heedless and opportunistic Gibson. A very bad month's work, Mel. Perhaps, though, he did us a favour. Nothing exposed the viciousness, the hate, the elephant-memory malevolence of Scottish nationalism quite like *Braveheart* did.

Colin Gilbert

In one of her short stories, Ali Smith describes a most unsavoury character: male, in his forties, expensively suited; lean and suave, she writes, 'and devilish, like a BBC executive'. We all recognise the type; tieless in his Paul Smith finery, discoursing opaquely about platforms, strategies and visions.

Which brings us to Colin Gilbert, producer of comedy television. Gilbert not only spent years as a BBC executive but is the son of a BBC executive too, Jimmy Gilbert, the Television Centre veteran behind *The Frost Report*, *Fawlty Towers* and *The Good Life*. Comedy, clearly, is the ancestral inheritance. Yet, Gilbert *fils* is scarcely of the breed described by Smith. Broad of beam and well-insulated against the onset of winter, with the bearing of a geology lecturer nearing retirement, Gilbert is neither lean nor suave. But he *is* devilish. Pandemically devilish. Few figures have gone about Scotland sowing misery and despair, horror and bafflement as Colin Gilbert has.

Steady on, you say: isn't he merely a maker of television entertainments? How could such weighty claims be advanced of a bloke in a revolving bow tie and size 17 shoes? Because Gilbert has used his powers so unwisely. He made, in the main, programmes that were not merely bad, but bad in ways that set the tone, that drew the blueprint. He designed a mask – but a mask, as Wilde wrote, that ate eventually into the face.

Born in Glasgow, Gilbert went south at a tender age to reunite with his father, then the BBC's Head of Comedy. Gilbert the Younger did some writing for radio, on *Weekending* and *The News Huddlines,* then in 1975 returned north to be a floor manager at BBC Scotland. Clearly a dynastic route was being cleared for young Gilbert, with floor-management as its apprenticeship. He returned to London to script-edit *Not The Nine O'Clock News* then, in 1983, went back to Glasgow to head up the Comedy Unit, BBC Scotland's light-entertainment department. It was a propitious time. Alternative comedy had just appeared, buttressed by the new Channel Four. With his impeccable connections Gilbert was on the inside track, producing a set of serviceable sketch shows – *A Kick Up The Eighties*, *Laugh??? I Nearly Paid My Licence Fee*, *Naked Video*.

They gave little hint of the horrors to come. Those would not seep through the cracks until 1988 and the inception of *Rab C Nesbitt*.

Whether in business or culture, the absence of competition is to be regretted. In Scotland particularly it resulted in broadcast comedy being wholly the province of the BBC. It proved too pricey for the nation's commercial channel. Comedy is the mirror in which a culture sees itself, particularly television comedy. Consider how it has captured the moods of contemporary Britain; from the Modernism of *Hancock's Half Hour*, through the satire of *That Was The Week That Was*, to the property-owning purgatories of *Bless This House* and *Love Thy Neighbour* and on to the nervous breakdowns of *Men Behaving Badly* and *The Office*. You may be of the opinion we are living through a comedic golden age, or you may stare at the screen blankly like a consultant just called to discuss your test results. Comedy is notoriously subjective. It is difficult to argue, though, that for half a century now Britain's television comedy has caught something of the sweep of this national narrative, like some electronic Bayeux Tapestry.

What, meanwhile, for more than half this span, has Gilbert the Younger been offering us? Well, crap, in the main: dreadful, gurning, witless crap; crap in kilts, crap in tenements, crap of every hue and consistency. You name it and Gilbert can render it dismal. Consider his legacy, inspect the CV, feel the width. It's shocking, this Gilbertian oeuvre of blitzed victims and cud-chewing retards, in shows such as *Athletico Partick*, *Empty*, *Legit*, *Dear Green Place* and so on. Look particularly at *Rab C Nesbitt*, possibly Gilbert's best-known show, the creation to which all else is footnote. The show charted the travails of a philosopher-prole, a grimy street-corner pariah. Nesbitt lived in a grief-hole of a flat in Govan with wife Mary Doll and sundry maladjusted offspring. Each week, in pubs, shopping centres and benefit offices, he aimed spittle-flecked rage at those he held responsible for his station in life. Nesbitt was essentially Alf Garnett on Jobseeker's Allowance, though with Garnett's chosen scapegoats – left-wingers and immigrants – supplanted by the English and the educated, both of which were recurring targets in Gilbert's shows. His tendencies deepened in 1996 when he removed his department, the Comedy Unit, from BBC control and established it as an independent production company. Effectively, Scottish broadcast comedy came under monopoly control, its character determined with Soviet implacability by the prejudices of Colin Gilbert, with his passions for football, Christmas-cracker humour, variety-hall knockabout and inner-city squalor.

For Gilbert seldom saw a gallery without wishing to play to it. His shows indulged every parochial, clannish, intolerant, taxi-driving twitch in the Scottish body politic. They promoted a view of west-of-Scotland working-class life in which the natives were little more than Uncle Toms, subservient to their addictions to alcohol and chips; always quarrelsome, always singing in the streets, always gruffly sentimental, always ready to remedy perceived slights with the issuing of a sore face. Gilbert's work was the screeching, vomiting equivalent of an A&E waiting room on a Bank Holiday weekend. Either that or it was just reliably, predictably lame; twenty years behind the curve, laugh-tracked and old-fashioned with a pride that implied those responsible, or culpable, were forcibly resisting acquaintance with new-fashioned. His shows were also stridently idiomatic and colloquial, to a point that they could be deciphered only by a small constituency of hardened Glaswegians.

Despite this, Gilbert nursed constantly a grievance that the BBC network, with colonialist hauteur, turned up its nose at his shows, ignoring conveniently the fact that he was making tabloid, red-top television, wholly emboldened by the want of competition, while depending slavishly upon a thinning gene pool of usual suspects, friends-of-friends and trusted fellow-travellers. One example was *Dear Green Place*, a sit-com about Glasgow park keepers that brought hitherto-unimagined shades of hilarity to the business of maintaining a sizable civic amenity. Or there was *In Voluntary*, set in a Highland charity chop. This starred Karen Dunbar and Julie Wilson Nimmo, wife of *Chewin' the Fat* star Greg Hemphill, whose comedy partner Ford Kiernan starred in *Dear Green Place*, written by an actor who appeared in *Chewin' the Fat* alongside Dunbar, whose one-woman series, like all others cited previously, was made by, yes, The Comedy Unit.

Happily, Gilbert is gone now; he sold out to the RDF media group in 2006. Hopefully it is not too late to recover. We are left, then, only to mourn what might have been, in those two unhappy decades of playground vulgarity and pub roughness. Imagine, if you will, *Only Fools and Horses* made for young offenders. That was what Colin Gilbert made for Scotland. And it was no laughing matter.

Sir Fred Goodwin

Some years back, on stage in Glasgow, the author and wit Clive James delivered his own take on the then-sizzling topic of disgraced former bank chief Sir Fred Goodwin, or as the red-tops had dubbed him, the 'Scumbag Millionaire'. After proposing a tombola in which the prizes would be a box of Ratners jewellery and 100,000 shares in the Royal Bank of Scotland, James recalled ruefully that recently he had taken out a potentially lucrative investment plan with the RBS-owned NatWest. The plan, a bank employee had told him jovially, would fail to pay out 'only if the entire western economic structure collapses'. Which, of course, it duly did.

And nobody copped the blame, in Britain at any rate, like Goodwin did. At the end of the noughties the banker became perhaps the most publically reviled Scot since Moors Murderer Ian Brady. His name was the stuff of stand-up routines and sit-com sketches, invoked whenever conversation turned to financial chicanery, vast wealth or the fall of the civilised world. It all got quite hysterical for a time. The Royal Bank of Scotland had required propping up by the government to the tune of £24 billion, a shortfall racked up principally on Goodwin's watch, through bad debts, ineffective rights issues and the disastrous purchase of the ABM Amro group.

In the aftermath, we learned that Goodwin, who had looked harmless enough with his tweeds and blond thatch, had run RBS with a manner that had been bombastic, reckless and vainglorious. All of this, however, seemed to bother the public less than the pay-off he'd salvaged from the wreckage, most particularly his RBS pension pot, estimated at £17 million. In the knockabout arena of public Punch and Judy, Goodwin cringed beneath the blows of the big collective stick, the words 'That's the way to do it!' ringing in his ears.

Or, at least, we assume he did. Sightings of Goodwin, then and since, have been few and far between. His was among the most comprehensive rustications our public life has yet witnessed. Only Lord Lucan has vanished from the scene so thoroughly. At one point one would not have been surprised if rustics with pitchforks were called upon to root him out.

His £3 million Edinburgh family mansion was targeted by miscreants who, it transpired later were connected to the quasi-anarchist organisation Bank Bosses Are Criminals. Three ground-floor windows were smashed, and the rear window of Sir Fred's Mercedes S600. 'This is just the beginning,' read an e-mail from the group, though they were never heard from again. 'Top fucking work comrades!' responded one sympathiser on his website. Goodwin was not at home but was reportedly 'shaken' by the attack. Yet it was essentially a proactive variation on a theme that was already growing insistent, that Sir Fred make reparation for the fiscal events of the past six months, for profiting so handsomely while the piggy-banks of RBS employees and British taxpayers were emptied. *Panorama* produced a documentary on his rise: 'Bankers will tell you they considered Goodwin a deity,' it explained. 'He believed himself the best banker, the best accountant and the best marketer there'd ever been, and he passed that confidence on to them. But the consensus now is that he came to believe his own hype.'

Demands mounted for Goodwin to forfeit everything but the fillings in his teeth. Twenty-one Labour MPs signed a Commons motion calling on the Queen to strip away his knighthood, awarded in 2004. MSPs investigated the possibility of using the Anti-Terrorism, Crime and Security Act of 2001 to seize Goodwin's home and collection of classic cars. An Edinburgh bookmaker ceased taking bets on whether Sir Fred would be compelled to relinquish some or all of his pension. Labour MSP Margaret Curran, meanwhile, proposed her so-called Goodwin's Tax, levied at 100 per cent, as a means of denying Sir Fred his pension and his lump-sum pay-offs. Even gamblers of more modest means got in on the game, with the appearance of Fat Cat Cash Back, an internet game in which players raced against the clock to claw back from Goodwin £100,000. His children were withdrawn from their Edinburgh private schools. His wife, formerly a stalwart of the Edinburgh social charity scene, ceased to attend events. Rumour proliferated. Goodwin could have been living with in-laws in Glasgow. He was moving perhaps to America or Melbourne. He would replace Max Mosley as head of Formula One's governing body. Or maybe, as one report claimed, not very believably, he and his family boarded a Globespan package-holiday flight from Edinburgh to Nice. Tabloid newspapers were thought to be offering £30,000 for the first snap of the errant banker. Matters reached their nadir truly when even Max Clifford, undiscriminating PR agent of barrel-scraping repute, declared that, if asked, he would not accept Goodwin as a client: 'Clearly he's frightened and he's keeping a low profile,' Clifford said. 'The problem is that any move on his part to defuse the anger felt for him, by handing back some of his pension, will be interpreted as a response to the attack on his house, which might give protesters licence to take more action against him. It will be extremely difficult to pull the situation back now.'

Goodwin addressed the situation, its cat's cradle of private greed and public responsibility, by not addressing it. The heat diminished in time but the banker never re-emerged. He remains utterly absent. Or perhaps not. Goodwin was a blood sacrifice. The rich hated him because he lost them money and the poor hated him because he had so much money himself. He became the escape valve for the collective anger towards the financial situation. He united the rich and the poor in their suffering. If you asked them, 90 per cent of the population, even yet, won't be happy until Goodwin is subjected to capital punishment. That can't happen, obviously, so the punishment became symbolic via the newspapers or on his house. Nobody, apart from a G20 protester, really wanted a class war. So Goodwin served the purpose of operating in its place. In a sense, it was quite useful that Goodwin was around. Just don't say so to Clive James.

Alex Harvey

When was popular music at its best, at its shining peak? A growing consensus thinks the answer obvious: 1971. This may seem counterintuitive given that by 1971 the glory days of The Beatles and The Rolling Stones were behind them and the pop explosion of the 1960s tailing off. The dawn of the 1970s was a time of anxiety and cultural recalibration, soured by burn-out and by a growing political radicalism. Clearly, something vital had passed. Yet from its ashes something other was being born, a more mature and varied form of popular music, proficient technically and emotionally evolved. In many ways, the 1970s were a golden age: they ran the gamut from David Bowie to Gary Numan, via progressive rock, reggae, confessional singer-songwriters, glam, punk, disco, new wave and ska. It must have been a glorious time to be young, amidst this kaleidoscopic swirl of innovation, augmented by its attendant youth cults and tribes. It almost certainly was. Except in Scotland. All thanks to Alex Harvey.

It is difficult at this distance to evoke just how stifling was Harvey's influence. As a performer the Glaswegian had marked theatrical tendencies but his music was undiluted heavy rock, hard and charmless, replete with screams, growls and screeching guitar solos. His songs boasted titles like 'Gang Bang' and 'Snake Bite' and sounded like a drum kit dropped on your head as a mental patient drove past in a juggernaut. Harvey himself, meanwhile, looked as though he'd been helping police with their enquiries, with missing teeth and hair like the innards of a barber's bin, his expression either stupefied or threatening. He was the lead vocalist as recidivist; as the scary, feral Glaswegian of common nightmare, fronting a bunch of tinnitus-ridden brickies.

The odd thing, though, was that it worked. From 1972 to 1978, The Sensational Alex Harvey Band were a major act; feted by the music press, fixtures on the *Old Grey Whistle Test*, a huge draw on the concert circuit. They even had several hit singles: *Delilah* in 1975 and *Boston Tea Party* the year following. SAHB made it to American radio and British bedroom walls, defined visually by their flamboyant guitarist Zal Cleminson in his clown make-up and its frontman in his trademark striped t-shirt, pleading and imploring, playing to the gallery like a tramp begging for coppers.

To the naked eye, though, all seemed most encouraging. From the backstreets of Glasgow had come, finally, Scotland's first rock star proper, a performer as rough and ready as the city that bred him, putting its straight-ahead spirit on the world map. What wasn't to like? Well, everything really. This was an inauspicious moment in the story of mainstream popular culture. Financial input from American film studios was being withdrawn. Cinemas were being converted into bingo halls. The collectivism of the 1960s was fragmenting. Television was resorting to smut. And popular music had bifurcated: on one hand into manufactured pop for teenagers and, on the other, heavy rock for the polytechnic crowd.

This was the context in which Harvey prospered. It was a realm he shared with Deep Purple, AC/ DC, Rainbow, Mountain, Nazareth, Status Quo, Ten Years After, Rory Gallagher and a hundred others; hairy headbanging men with faces sculpted from chilled lard, who sang in growly tones that suggested they'd been constipated since the late 1950s. Their genre prioritised the music's impact upon its audience, its power and volume, its physical heft. It dwelt in student unions and shabby concert halls and was consumed by ugly, sexually thwarted white guys in combat jackets and army greatcoats. Britain endured a good few years of this rubbish, until New Wave and racial diversity combined to impede its progress.

While it prospered, though, the style exerted a curious geographic spread. On the hard rock circuit in Britain, Harvey and his band were leading lights. In Scotland, however, they were messiahs, partly because they were local boys made good and partly because the music's elementary and unsophisticated nature echoed Scotland's conceit of itself. It was pie-and-potato, bitter-beer rock for straightforward blokes, with none of that effeminate David Bowie stuff. It wasn't tricksy progressive rock for university graduates. There was a dismaying logic to this prejudice. What else would beguile the artless labourers of Dundee or Perth or Montrose like rock that was as loud, basic and beery as those who listened to it?

And so it was that one style of music came to dominate, nay tyrannise, Scotland. It was, quite literally, the only show in town. Soon, Harvey was joined by acolytes and imitators. The merciful amnesia of history has erased many other names of the period, such as Chou Pahrot, Stallion, Stone The Crows, Beggars' Opera and Scheme. Each and all were shudderingly horrible. Although in their late teens and early twenties, the musicians seemed wreathed with the seedy fatigue of drunken uncles. They shared an aesthetic best described as convict-on-day release: grown-out feather cuts, impulsive tattoos, dental mishaps, charity shop leather jerkins, seldom of the correct size. The music was no more charming, just witless concatenations of power chords and lyrical cliché, focused usually on witchy, double-dealing chicks.

Effectively, for nearly a decade, Scotland was obliged to call a halt to its popular music, all because Harvey and his sensational minstrels had chanced upon a magic formula, for creating music as rudimentary and charmless as the audience it serviced. It was music that in Scotland rendered all competition redundant. Elsewhere in Britain audiences were growing familiar with new and innovative rock acts like Sparks and Roxy Music and Hawkwind; while in Scotland the bill of fare comprised exclusively of hairy duffers like Tear Gas and Rosetta Stone. It took until 1980 for the curse to lift. By the time of his death two years later, Harvey's work was an unhappy memory. He is remembered now for his impact rather than his contribution. The latter left Scottish popular music between a rock and a hard place indeed.

Jim Kerr

n 1980, the American rock critic Greil Marcus delivered a famously damning verdict. It dealt with Rod Stewart, the sandpaper-throated, tartan-bedecked purveyor of raunchy rock anthems: 'Rarely has a singer had as full and unique a talent as Rod Stewart,' Marcus wrote. 'Rarely has anyone betrayed his talent so completely. Once the most compassionate presence in music, he has become a bilious self-parody – and sells more records than ever.' The finding was not incorrect. For rock fans, even today, it remains a matter of real regret that in the mid-1970s Stewart abandoned his melodic, autobiographic folk-pop for music of a less enchanting variety; pounding, squawking rock, made to be heard on car radios and in sports arenas, while chaps named Chip or Chuck balanced on their shoulders their topless cheerleader girlfriends. Marcus had Rod Stewart bang to rights. But the pineapple-haired performer was by no means a lone culprit. More recently, another Caledonically-connected singer has mimicked Stewart's trajectory, from early promise to mature brilliance, followed by a flailing descent into a bubbling vat of kitsch.

That singer is Jim Kerr, the balloon-faced, blouson-wearing frontman of a band from Glasgow named Simple Minds. Now, there once was a time when Simple Minds were genuinely impressive. They did something few Scottish rock groups had done before,

they stirred into their music ingredients that were fresh and arresting: the Germanic electronica of Kraftwerk, the icy funk of Sly and the Family Stone. Not for them the lumbering rock music that had prevailed in the city. Simple Minds were exotic and enigmatic, a new wave update of Bowie and Roxy Music, with music that explored glittering night-time cityscapes. They were feted critically and successful commercially. In short, they were properly good.

And then something happened: namely U2. Throughout the early 1980s, the Irish four-piece and its intense, wiry music had been growing in stature. By 1984, the band were set to make their breakthrough in America, necessitating for them a bigger, more emotive sound, duly delivered on albums like *The Joshua Tree* and *Rattle and Hum*. When this approach started paying dividends somewhere in the collective Simple Minds brain box the penny, or perhaps the quarter, dropped. The Glasgow band and U2 shared a number of affinities. Each had Celtic roots. Each produced music that looked to the horizons, that prowled over landscapes of gorse and rain. Neither shied from showmanship or bombast.

And so, from around 1984 onwards, Simple Minds began to change. Jekyll became Hyde. Sublime turned ridiculous, just as it had with Rod Stewart, for similar reasons and by similar mechanisms. Suddenly, a band meant for chaps who appreciated guitar effects, raincoats and songs about *der Autobahn* went starspangled. The band's taut, arty rock swelled with the steroids of Stateside affectation. They performed the theme song of the bratpack flick *The Breakfast Club*. They took to wearing pixie boots and loose-fitting chiffon coat things in primary colours. Their music became bloated, forceful and obvious. They adopted transatlantic accents. Or, rather, Jim Kerr did. Who cares what the other four did? Few bands have been associated so exclusively with their singer; not, in this case, because said singer was inherently fascinating but because the other members made tailor's dummies look like gay Marines. And yet. The efficacy of their plan can be inferred from one fact: that while U2 remain among the most adored and money-spinning acts in show business history Simple Minds have just played the free New Year's Eve concert in Edinburgh.

It would be easy to blame this bathos on Jim Kerr, and this is no reason to avoid doing so. He always has been the silliest of men. Of course, the vocalists of rock bands aimed at students and teenagers seldom have the gravitas of clerics, but even by the debased standards of the field Kerr was exceptional. For starters, he was screamingly, punchably pretentious; compared to Kerr, second-year sociology students came over like Albanian bin-men. The *New Musical Express* used to run an item in which musicians listed their cultural passions. This is Kerr's contribution, from December, 1981: 'Books: *Alexander Platz* by Alfred Döbin, *Labyrinths* by Jorge Luis Borges and *Amerika* by Franz Kafka. Films by Völker, Visconti and anything by Laurel and Hardy. Heroes: great liars, great thieves and various assassins. Favourite events: seeing an angel and the Moon landing.' No matter how you try you will never be able to unread the previous paragraph.

Matters only got worse following the Live Aid concerts of July 1985. The multi-continental charity event fired a starting pistol on conspicuous empathy amid the rock community. Before we knew it the types of artists famed for polishing their boots on their servants' faces were trekking to Addis Ababa to hold forth on their humbleness. U2 threw their weight behind the project, which meant, inevitably, that space in the jeep needed freeing up for Jim Kerr and his aching conscience. This period in the mid-1980s resembled some bizarre mass delusion, a modern-day tulip mania, with Kerr as lead botanist. Swiftly, he broadened his portfolio of single-issues, to encompass any problem whose solution was eluding the men in charge from Northern Ireland, in 'Belfast Child', to South Africa, with 'Mandela Day' and 'Biko'.

Since the fall of Communism and the sudden unpopularity of eye make-up for men, things have been quieter for the Minds. For two decades now they have loitered in career limbo: part Eighties nostalgia act, part delusional old troupers who won't take the hint. Their concerts can be uneasy melds of each mode. Can there be a more melancholy sight in the world than fans absenting a concert hall when some lame, indulgent slab of tosh from a justifiably obscure recent album is smuggled in between the hits? Yes there can. It is convoys of white stretch limos outside the venue; hired, beyond doubt, by married couples anticipating a nostalgic party evening, then obliged to suffer unfamiliar material because the band were determined to demonstrate they remain a vital creative force. There should be some manner of trades description legislation against this. If you're a performer over forty you accept your audience wishes to hear only the songs that have been embossed on their synapses. This may not be artistically satisfying for the performer but their cut on the £30 ticket price should provide some comfort.

Instead, Kerr and the Minds pursue a kind of tit-for-tat arrangement whereby a 'classic' is traded for some piece of windy nonsense from the band's recent twilight albums. This occasionally serves to remind what an interesting, supple band the Minds once were. If Rod Stewart can manage the feat, so can Simple Minds and their preposterous, over-inflated frontman.

Dr Samuel Johnson

As inventor of the English dictionary, Dr Samuel Johnson knew of what he spoke. He is described in the Dictionary of National Biography as 'the most distinguished man of letters in English history'. Ruskin wrote that in Johnson he 'at once and for ever recognised a man entirely sincere, and infallibly wise in the view and estimate he gave of the common questions, business and ways of the world', which was nice. In *Anecdotes of the Late Samuel Johnson*, Hester Thrale's festschrift of 1786, the writer recounted a debate between Johnson and a Scottish *émigré* wishing to know one thing: how the good Doctor regarded the land from which the *émigré* hailed. 'It is a very vile country, to be sure, Sir,' Johnson replied. And yet, countered his inquisitor, God made it. 'Certainly he did,' said Johnson. 'But we must always remember that he made it for Scotchmen.'

As in old variety routines, the drumroll and cymbal crash were almost audible. Les Dawson had mothers-in-law; Bernard Manning had ethnic minorities: Samuel Johnson had the Scots, and Scotland. They were his fall-guys, horses he seldom missed a chance to whip. In the salons and coffee houses of Georgian London the table was set upon a roar ceaselessly as the good Doctor dispensed withering verdicts upon the wild, uncharted nation to the north: 'Knowledge was divided among the Scots like bread in a besieged town,' he

would say. 'To every man a mouthful, to no man a bellyful.' Or 'Your country consists of two things, stone and water. There is, indeed, a little earth above the stone in some places, but a very little; and the stone is always appearing. It is like a man in rags; the naked skin is still peeping out.'

Putting this latter objection to one side, though, in 1773 Johnson undertook a three-month tour of Scotland and the Western Isles, accompanied by James Boswell, his Scots-born friend and biographer. The pair visited Edinburgh, St Andrews, Aberdeen, Inverness, Skye, Raasay, Coll, Mull, and Glasgow. Twelve years later Johnson recounted the visit in *Journal of a Tour of the Hebrides.* The trip was not purely recreational, of course. It was intended also to enhance through direct experience Johnson's store of prejudice, to freshen the repartee he'd been polishing over the previous four decades. By this time the writer was sixty-three-years-old and prone intermittently to tuberculosis, scrofula, obsessive-compulsive behaviour, testicular cancer, pulmonary fibrosis, gout, hypertension, depression and Tourette syndrome. Seldom do any of these conditions enhance a visit to Portree.

Thus was it, then, that Scotland came to assume a singular, and bleakly ironic, status in the annals of travel. The most renowned tourist to explore the place – Dr Samuel Johnson, the writer quoted most after Shakespeare, the wisest wit of his age – loathed it. And famously so; some of Johnson's opinions of Scotland are in his rhetorical greatest hits. The most famed, perhaps, is the claim quoted in Boswell's *Life Of Johnson*, that 'the noblest prospect a Scotchman ever sees, is the high road that leads him to England!'

Running close second is his dictionary's definition of oats: 'A grain, which in England is generally given to horses, but in Scotland supports the people.' Or perhaps this broadside, recorded by Mrs Thrale: 'Seeing Scotland, Madam, is only seeing a worse England. It is seeing the flower gradually fade away to the naked stalk.'

All this begs the question why Johnson nursed such disdain for Scotland anyway. Fashion, really: such an antipathy was all the rage then. In the latter half of the 18th century anti-Scottish sentiment flourished at every level of English society; royally, institutionally and anecdotally. Partly this was a backlash to Scottish success, as a legion of capable Scots flooded south: James Thomson, the nature poet (and, amusingly, author of 'Rule Britannia'), the Earl of Bute, tutor of the king and, later, prime minister, portraitist Allan Ramsay, Robert and James Adam, architects. With anti-Scottish sentiment Johnson was merely the starriest proponent; a sort of Georgian Jeremy Clarkson ('This is the best sedan chair . . . *in the world.*'). Another cause was Jacobitism, the lemon-sucking philosophy that sought to supplant the Hanoverian line of succession with a restored Stuart dynasty. Controversially, the former – think gouty nutters in big wigs, or Hugh Laurie in *Blackadder III* – advocated an informal relationship between parliament and monarchy, while the Stuarts – think Mad McAdder in the same series – preferred the citizenry to sit up straight and keep its feet off the furniture. The Highland clans, seldom slow to rouse if skulls were likely to be axed, stood behind the Jacobites, only to be routed by the armies of the Duke of Cumberland at Culloden.

On the *realpolitik* of the situation Johnson was ambivalent: 'I cannot now curse the House of Hanover,' he told Boswell, 'nor would it be decent for me to drink King James' health in the wine that King George gave me money to pay for.' He wasn't so reticent when it came to the comic potential of the resulting Scotophobia. The reaction against Jacobitism ensured this had no shortage of pretexts. Scotland was depicted commonly as a haven of cannibalism, notoriously through the legend of Sawney Bean. Hogarth in his art lampooned the Scots. In the Whig press Scotland's affinity with France played poorly. Inserted into the national anthem was a verse exhorting Marshal Wade to crush 'rebellious Scots'. Jacobitism became the prism through which England focused its irritation on Scotland's 'otherness'.

In the circumstances, it was hardly surprising Johnson so little enjoyed his tour of the Western Isles. The Highlands had been only recently depopulated by the Clearances; the clan system was being dismantled by Act of Parliament. Privateers and slave ships patrolled the coasts, searching for victims. Scotland's forests were in the midst of being wiped from the land. Away from the main settlements daily life cleaved to the manners of centuries past. In some ways Johnson was scandalised: 'Some method to stop this epidemic desire of wandering', he wrote, 'which spreads its contagion from valley to valley, ought to be sought with great diligence.' Yet, in more ways, he was not. Baiting the Scots was his party piece and a cornerstone of his fame. He returned from his travels better informed than ever, and perhaps touched even by the gallows humour that is a Scotsman's birthright: 'After having seen the deaf taught arithmetick,' Johnson wrote at the end of his journey following a visit to a school for the hard of hearing, 'who would be afraid to cultivate the Hebrides?'

Can it be said honestly that Johnson and his influence on Scotland was malign? Are we conflating opinion with outcome? Possibly. It has to be conceded that in some ways Johnson was clearly of benefit to the Scots; in the Ossian affair, for example. In 1760 the Scottish writer James Macpherson began to publish an epic cycle of poems based, he claimed, upon a treasury of rediscovered Gaelic folklore, composed by the warrior bard Ossian in the third century. The cycle became a sensation. Napoleon

Bonaparte and Thomas Jefferson were said to be admirers. It was translated into Hungarian, Polish, Italian, Russian, French and German; an extract featured in *The Sorrows of Young Werther* by Goethe. And then Johnson turned his attentions upon them. He was not impressed. More crucially, he was not convinced. Asked whether he believed any man of the time could write such poetry Johnson replied: 'Yes. Many men. Many women. And many children.' The cycle, declared Johnson, was not authentic: the language that Macpherson claimed to have translated had never been a written language. Johnson played a central role in a groundswell that, eventually, would see Ossian declared a fake. The consensus has held firm since. That groundswell was most propitious: had the poems gone unchallenged they surely would have nourished the well of nonsense used to irrigate the plains of monomania tended by swivel-eyed nationalists like MacDiarmid and his inheritors.

Here too, Scotland has basked in reflected glory; with Boswell, for instance. Something in the Scottish psyche is tickled by knowledge that the biographer, confidant and companion, the mucker, the best mate of perhaps the most considerable figure in literary history was a plump depressive Calvinist from Edinburgh. The knowledge gratified that old Scottish suspicion: that the worst of us is equal to the best of them, the *them* here being the English. This rather overlooks the fact that Boswell was the son of a judge, Lord Auchinleck, and thus only slightly less privileged than, say, the Duke of Kent. But, tish and fie; Boswell was playing with the big boys, so hurrah for us. Brought to mind is the scene in *Trainspotting* where Sick Boy unpicks the significance of the tryst between Ursula Andress and James Bond. Like Bond, Boswell was king for the day, a proxy, representing the entirety of his countrymen: 'Ursula Andress, the quintessential Bond girl,' says Sick Boy. 'That's what everyone says. The embodiment of his superiority over us. Beautiful, exotic, highly sexual and totally unavailable to anyone apart from him. Shite. Let's face it. She can shag one punter from Edinburgh, she'd shag the lot of us.'

So, in certain ways, Scotland derived benefit from its connections to the titan of English letters. In other ways it did not. Johnson helped nurture a Scottish trait that later would blossom like a triffid: victimhood. The contemporaneous Highland Clearances fed into this, as did the implosion of Jacobitism. In the late 1700s, to be Scottish was no walk in the park. The response to these attacks, as the 18th and 19th centuries proceeded, contained a bleak logic: if Scotland was to be victimised, Scots would withhold the satisfaction of letting its persecutors see that it bothered them. The iron entered the soul. A carapace grew on the Scottish mindset. Like a Whitehall guardsman, it would not react. It mattered not that Sir Walter Scott was infantilising the culture of the clans for foreign consumption or that, from Darien to Thatcher, Scotland seemed to be getting the stickier end of the lollipop. In its impassive, square-jawed, fist-clenched way Scotland could take it. The nation had been inured to criticism by sarcasm and satire.

The sharpest of it had fallen from the lips and the pen of Dr Samuel Johnson. He conjured a vision of a crude, uncultured, pointlessly proud Scotland, a place of dreadful food, unlettered natives, unrealistic ambition and of almost cosmic misfortune. In many ways, the good Doctor was dispensing self-fulfilling prophecies. And Scotland has been living down to them ever since.

Eric Joyce

The Scottish predilection for alcohol is infamous. Mention Scotland to an outsider, particularly in Britain, and booze will be among the first things they think of. The sozzled Scot is the stuff of caricature and stereotype, of music-hall joke and sit-com quip, whether he is ebullient on the terraces of a football ground or slumped in a Kings Cross doorway, muttering about the government. All nations, one supposes, have their hook, their motif. Bring up lederhosen and we see Germans marching towards bratwurst. With France, the picture changes to stripey jerseys and baguettes. Scandanavians: either Vikings or sexpot blondes. Italians: gropers on mopeds.

And each of these cultures has its own relationship with alcohol, generally a convivial relationship, designed to enhance social interaction. In Scotland, this latter aspect pertains only partially. The Scottish drinker is, on the whole, indifferent as to whether others accompany him. His relationship with alcohol is intense and personal. It is a one-on-one thing, as with the consumption of narcotics.

Alcohol, believes the Scot, has a job to do; a load to lift. Anthropologists term it fire-gazing, this propensity for sitting in bars, imbibing, staring into space. We find expressions of the tendency in Scottish literature going way back, most famously in

Burns and his 'drouthy neibors'. MacDiarmid's 'A Drunk Man Looks at The Thistle' is central. But perhaps the defining summary, the account that sealed the deal, was 'I Belong to Glasgow', written by Will Fyffe in 1930, a song sung by a reeling, delusional drunk as he tumbled into his cups: 'I'm only a common old working chap/ As anyone here can see,' the lyrics went, 'But when I get a couple o' drinks on a Saturday/Glasgow belongs to me!' It is this intimacy, this para-social aspect of the relationship with drink that causes the difficulties. For the drinking Scot little else gets a look-in. Alcohol, in a sense, is Scotland's medicine.

But, often, it is bad medicine; medicine with regrettable side effects, namely melancholia and aggression. And this is where we bid welcome to Eric Joyce, Member of Parliament for Falkirk. Prior to Joyce's notoriety, beginning in 2008, it seemed the archetypal drunken Scotsman had disappeared for a spell. We'd seen him last perhaps in the shape of Charles Kennedy, former leader of the Liberal Democrats, brought low by alcoholism. Kennedy is instructive here. He was yin to the yang presented by Joyce, a quiet, reflective drunk, a hobby toper.

His decline was painful to watch, even if there was plenty of time in which to watch it, so protracted was the process; three years from rumour to resignation. Rumours of his 'ill health' began doing the rounds in 2003 when he missed several debates on Iraq. His leadership style was criticised too, characterised as it was by a certain tickled levity or readiness to present himself as what he was, a quick-witted Highland boy with little patience for Westminster politesse. And then, as always in Scottish affairs, it got worse. Once word was out and we knew what to look for we found it in Kennedy's pallor and his casual way with the finer points of policy detail. A dismal display in 2005 at the launch of the Lib-Dem manifesto was put down to a late night attending the birth of his first child. The excuses, though, ran out quickly as it became painfully evident Kennedy was familiar with malt whisky to an extent his responsibilities as a Highland MP did not warrant. At this time he appeared to be walking a lonely, joyless road. Like the character in 'I Belong to Glasgow', Kennedy internalised his dependencies, whereupon they mastered him.

At the other end of the scale, meanwhile, is Eric Joyce, rambunctious hellraiser of this parish. There was little that was maudlin about Joyce, at least not to begin with. In the Scottish vernacular is a most applicable term: *steaming*. It is a description of the state of inebriation, deriving from the word steamboats, suggesting a considerable and possibly reckless forward momentum. The term evokes well what we know of Joyce's various interludes of shame. In 2010 he was arrested for failing to provide a breath test, fined and banned from driving for a year. Two years later he was described as having gone 'berserk' in the Palace of Westminster, punching Conservative MP Stuart Andrew, hitting Phil Wilson, Labour Assistant Whip, and turning on two other MPs as they attempted to restrain him. Joyce admitted he had been 'hammered'. He was suspended from the Labour party and continued serving his constituents as an independent.

Then, in March 2013, Joyce was removed by Metropolitan Police officers following a brawl in a bar in the Palace of Westminster. Newspapers ran witness accounts and mobile phone pictures of Joyce being removed in a headlock and sat upon by officers: 'I can vividly remember a policeman's hat rolling on the ground towards me,' reported an onlooker. Subsequently Joyce was banned from being served alcohol in each of parliament's eight licensed premises. He refuses to stand down and says he will not relinquish his seat until the next general election.

Square of jaw and brusque of bearing, with a reputation as

catnip to the ladies, Joyce was a private in the Black Watch before serving in the Royal Army Educational Corps, departing at the rank of major. Perhaps this is why he keeps falling into trouble. For whatever reason, probably film and television depictions, we find something faintly comedic in the designation of Major, particularly when the bearer is rolling on the floor with the Metropolitan Police, straining to land a punch. No doubt Joyce would argue his background cuts him some slack, sets him apart from the featherweights on Civvy Street, leaves him some goodwill to exhaust. It could be argued just as easily that the converse is true. What does remain beyond debate is that an old position has a new incumbent; that just as the drunken Scotsman archetype was falling into disuse, along came Joyce to shout incomprehensibly at passing traffic while brushing sick from his sleeve. Next stop for the galloping Major that doorway in Kings Cross?

James Kelman

'It is never difficult,' wrote the blessed Wodehouse famously, 'to distinguish between a Scotsman with a grievance and a ray of sunshine.' Few bear out the truth of this like James Kelman, author and activist of this parish. This not a man with whom to embark upon a month-long camping holiday. Kelman's writing is cheerless, sour, disgruntled and austere to an extent that scandalises even the Scots. His public bearing is less light-hearted still. From personal experience I confirm Kelman, a lean, thin-lipped Glaswegian approaching his seventies, embodies the old truism about the truly downhearted; that when they join the company it feels like someone just left it. The man is a raincloud in trousers. He has yet to purchase a pair of shoes not containing within an irritating little stone (or as he would no doubt put it, *a wee stane*). Reading his novels, written usually in a stream-of-consciousness, outlining with remorseless monomania the cosmic disappointments of sundry hapless, bedraggled Glaswegians, is as thrillingly sensuous as lining one's underwear with damp newsprint. His books are the literary equivalents of seeing a tramp engage in a fistfight with some bin men. They are not novels in the way that, say, *The Great Gatsby* or *Keep The Aspidistra Flying* are novels. They are buttonholing, spittle-flecked disquisitions that demand to know why you, as a reader, wish anything as soft-headed, as irredeemably bourgeois as mere entertainment anyway. *You utter prick.*

Why is Kelman like this? Well, because like so many bores and despots down the ages, he feels he is entitled to be, on the grounds he has been charged with a cause, a crusade, a Higher Mission. Its nature is linguistic. Kelman is soundly, nay aggressively, of the opinion that Scots should *and must* speak in the dialects that come to them naturally, with all their expletives, their colloquialisms, their particular local orthographies, their demotic sense of self. For example, this passage from *How Late It Was, How Late* (1994): 'He was here, he was leaning against auld rusty palings, with pointed spikes, some missing or broke off. And he looked again and saw it was a wee bed of grassy weeds, that was what he sitting on. His feet were back in view. He studied them; he wearing an auld pair of trainer shoes for fuck sake where had they come from he had never seen them afore man auld fucking trainer shoes. The laces were-nay even tied!'

Now, the readiness of Scots to speak in the accents with which they were born, employing locutions of a vibrant nature, is seldom in doubt, as will be confirmed by anyone who has flaunted an injudiciously chosen scarf at an Old Firm match. Kelman's writing has dealt occasionally with schoolteachers, so we might assume he has complaints in this direction, might suspect that teachers are imperial agents, charged with suppressing idiomatic speech in favour of something more resembling Received Pronunciation, just as Victorian headmasters punished pupils who dared employ their left hands. This is paranoia, of course, and utterly unverifiable. Teachers have a duty of care to impart correct, collectively settled information. So it is rather difficult to see Kelman's point here. Not that you'd rush to express this to him. He practises that old chestnut of the zealous mind: if you disagree with him it is because you too have been infected with the virus he seeks to eliminate.

We shift, anyway, to the second plank of Kelman's disgruntlement, that authors who think and behave as he does, with a defiant bias towards their Scottish roots and territory, are obliged *ad nauseam* – in newspapers and on television, at academic conferences, in scholarly treatises – to justify their actions, in the way someone in police custody might be obliged to explain repeatedly why he was carrying a crowbar at four in the morning. The presumption against Kelman is invariably one of guilt, he implies. Here is how he put the case in a Scottish Sunday newspaper in December 2012: 'Writers like myself are guilty of being "too Scottish"; our "Scottishness" is an attack on "Britishness" and acts as a disqualification. It is assumed that Scottish experience is homogeneous whereas English experience offers a wide-ranging and worldly heterogeneity. Our work is attacked in pseudo-literary tones for its perceived insularity. This also happens within Scotland; Anglocentric Scottish critics condemn Scottish writers for their "lack of diversity".'

With the best will in the world, it is difficult to consider such statements anything but radioactive eyewash. The view is just so painfully outdated. It may have possessed a degree of truth when Kelman was striving to make his reputation, in the early 1970s. Back then, the patrician Bedford Square model of publishing in Britain remained largely intact, with its preference for donnish, Literature and Society novels by the likes of Iris Murdoch and Doris Lessing, or the adultery-in-Hampstead fiction of, say, Andrea Newman. All that, though, was to wither in the face of wider social change: the emergence of ethnic voices and perspectives, of stylistic experimentation. All was pointing towards the birth of a new breed and this duly happened, with the inception in 1983 of

Granta 7, a cadre of young British novelists united by a desire to blaze new trails, or trails as new as their vile, privileged backgrounds would allow. Rapidly, authors were becoming celebrities: 'Now, if you're not careful,' wrote member Martin Amis in 1993, 'you can spend half your life being interviewed or photographed or answering questions posed by the press, on the telephone, about Fergie or Maastricht or your favourite colour.'

This is something akin to the position in which Kelman too finds himself; taking up broadsheet spreads to tell us how ignored and marginalised he feels. The world, he harrumphs, has failed to notice that his megaphone was manufactured in Kirkcaldy and is not one of those inferior English megaphones. Meanwhile, the landscape has changed and changed utterly. Now in order to secure media exposure, being Scottish is, if anything, a palpable advantage. A number of authors helped ensure this: Alasdair Gray with his unignorable literary and artistic phantasmagoria; Irvine Welsh and his urban horror shows; the melancholia of AL Kennedy; the extravagant fictions of Iain Banks; the hysteric existentialism of Janice Galloway; and, yes, even by the traduced and bypassed victim-king James Kelman; winner in 1994, lest we forget, of one of the shiniest baubles on the EngLit tree, the Booker Prize.

In the modern day Scottish language and writing are in no meaningful sense suppressed; certainly not within Scotland nor in England either, where a trace of imperial guilt has, in fact, ensured it an overly fair shake of the stick. In the pages of the *Guardian* and the *Daily Telegraph*, on BBC Two's *The Culture Show*, on Radio Four and Sky Arts, Scottish literature is admired and feted, its practitioners congratulated for extending the canon in authentic and compelling ways. Perhaps it is worth remembering that while the *Granta* list of 1983 contained no Scottish authors, in 2003 it featured three: A.L. Kennedy, Alan Warner and Andrew O'Hagan.

Put this to Kelman and he'd mumble grudgingly about Scottish writers being bought off with English gold, a process into which he perhaps gained some insight when he accepted his Booker.

In essence, then, Kelman's ill-tempered claims can be falsified by everyone with an interest except, it would appear, newspaper hacks with a deadline. Education authorities frown on slovenly speech not because they are engaged upon some programme of tacit ethnic cleansing but because it is ugly and incorrect. If Kelman has been attacked for being 'too Scottish' this happened in a vanished past. Nobody these days assumes Scottish experience is homogeneous or insular. Such attitudes have not been held for decades. And this is rather the point. Kelman is quite an old bloke now. He hangs on to his pain like a tearful divorce. He is the Florence Nightingale of nursed grievances. Perhaps he should read more P.G. Wodehouse.

R.D. Laing

.D. Laing was the doctor who put the psycho into psycho-
analyst. His fame, or notoriety, has survived not only death
but professional and personal discredit as a variation on the Mad
Psychiatrist meme: that of the mad, drunk, Scottish psychiatrist.
Search YouTube with his name and you will find hardly a single
TV clip or lecture-room video where Laing is not somewhere on
the Seven Dwarfs spectrum of the nightmare drinker; from Happy
to Sleepy via Dopey and Grumpy, though always, of course, Doc.
The father of anti-psychiatry, he was the best-known brain doctor
after Freud and Jung but also the classic case of the physician who
could not heal himself.

Long after his fortune-cookie poetry, his hippie-fascist hatred
of family and society, and his abject failure as a clinician have
slipped into merciful obscurity, the main association the phrase
'Scottish psychiatrist' conjures up is still with this tetchy narcissist;
who believed insanity was an oppressive social construct, who
encouraged schizophrenics to wallow in their own excrement,
discouraged all drug-based treatment for mental illness except
involuntary dosing with LSD, and was struck off the medical
register over complaints of drunkenness and violence.

He was, strange to think, a countercultural hero in the Britain
of the 1960s, a fixture of the Sunday supplements and of those

late-night TV panel discussions on which participants were allowed to smoke or, if so moved, to attack Bernard Levin. Laing got further into the spirit of things by appearing while titanically inebriated. As feted as Mick Jagger or Paul McCartney, Laing was the psychiatric equivalent of the crescendo to The Beatles' 'A Day in the Life'; discordant, chaotic, unpleasant but with a philosophy that held it was the patient's preference for harmony that had got them into this mess in the first place. One single tenet dominated Laing's thought: that our families can drive us mad. Were you to have shown Laing a distraught and dribbling malcontent he would have claimed they'd been unhinged not by grief or dislocation or any of the standard causes but by the psychological warfare waged within their domestic family unit; by the passive-aggression of mother, say; by father's terse annoyance; by the jockeying for position seen among siblings. It was the drip-drip effect of such emotional attrition, Laing thought, that filled the asylums.

Laing knew whereof he spoke. The family he raised were like first drafts; abandoned, torn up and tossed in the waste-paper basket. If it is our kith and kin that drive us to madness Laing was in Formula One, cackling maniacally inside his helmet. He fathered ten children by four women. The first five he abandoned and left in penury. Laing's daughter Karen once claimed he beat her so severely her brothers needed to intervene. Another daughter, Susan, died of leukemia at twenty-one. Laing insisted, against the wishes of her mother and siblings, that Susan be told of her diagnosis and at her funeral provoked a fist-fight with her social worker for disagreeing. Adam Laing, an alcoholic depressive, died at forty-one, of a heart attack, in a tent in a Spanish field. Another son, Adrian, produced a biography of his father: 'Being the son of R.D. Laing was neither amazing nor enlightening,' he wrote. 'For most of the time it was a crock of shit.'

The child was the father of the man. Laing was born in 1927 and grew up in the south of Glasgow in a repressed middle-class Presbyterian family; his cold and distant mother, he claimed, was opposed deeply to all displays of physical affection and would stick pins into his effigy. Laing graduated as a doctor from Glasgow University and joined an army psychiatric unit where he developed the thesis which would underpin his career, that schizophrenia and mental illness are treated best not with drugs but with empathy and concern; the so-called talking cure. Although it took him several further years to qualify as a psychiatrist – held up, he claimed in his generous fashion, by 'a whole hierarchy of idiots and mediocrities' – he never failed to stress his erudition and became a stranger to modesty; one colleague recalled Laing would say he was 'the only person in the world who spoke ancient Greek with a Glasgow accent'.

He set up a consultancy in Wimpole Street and embarked upon his glory years, when his insistence on letting it all hang out psychologically chimed neatly with the spirit of swinging London. It transpired Laing possessed an almost Doolittle-like ability to communicate with the traumatised. He treated Sean Connery, as recalled afterwards by the actor's wife Diane Cilento: 'He demanded a great deal of money, complete privacy, a limo to transport him to and from the meeting, and a bottle of the best single-malt Scotch at each session,' she wrote. Laing then established the Philadelphia Association, a treatment centre based in east London. He presided over a facility where psychiatrists outnumbered patients and casual sex was prescribed freely: 'Ronnie would be pompousing about dressed in white robes looking like Jesus,' recalled a visitor; 'I'd be asking him, "Why has that bloke got his hands all over that girl?" The whole thing stank.'

The 1970s were the crack-up. Depressed by the fading of his

celebrity, Laing grew desperate, branching into the 'politics of the birth process'. He set up rebirthing workshops and took to shamanism. He pursued a career as a poet, to widespread derision. Several marriages, familial bonds and the last remnants of his credibility were splashed against the porcelain. In 1984 Laing was arrested for throwing a bottle of wine through the window of the Bhagwan Shree Rajneesh Centre in Hampstead; the perfect symbolic encapsulation of a career which had veered between extreme personal recklessness and quasi-mystic eyewash. Three years later Laing was struck off the Medical Register for abusing a patient in a consultation and being caught in possession. He died in 1989 after collapsing on a tennis court in St Tropez.

And today he is all-but forgotten, or remembered as just an unsettling figure on the diorama of the kooky, credulous 1960s, alongside characters like Emil Savundra, Timothy Leary and Michael X. Laing's central idea – that madness is merely a set of observable symptoms rather than an underlying condition – lost all credibility decades ago. Until it did, thousands suffered no doubt by exposure to its faddish hysteria, to the psychological equivalent of blood-letting and trepanning.

Sir Harry Lauder

Sometime in the 1940s, the American entertainer Danny Kaye was fulfilling an engagement at the old Empire Theatre in Glasgow when he discovered that nearby resided Sir Harry Lauder. For Kaye this was big news. For over almost half a century Lauder had been a titan of the variety stage, in America as much as Britain, adored for his stirring songs and his insistence on performing in full Highland regalia, with sporran and Tam o' Shanter. As a former coal miner, Lauder's achievements had been astonishing. At one time he'd been the highest-paid entertainer in the world; a performer who'd topped the bill at the first Royal Command Performance; the first recording artist to sell a million records.

A meeting was arranged and Kaye was taken by chauffeur to Lauder's home in Strathaven, fifteen miles south. The pair got along famously and on Kaye's leaving Lauder announced he wished to make a presentation. Reverently, an old and knobbly walking stick was produced, seemingly the stick that for decades had been Lauder's on-stage trademark. A humbled Kaye thanked his host profusely and on the journey back marvelled aloud that such a piece of show business treasure was now his own. In the rear-view mirror the chauffeur eyed Kaye warily. Not quite, he countered. For Lauder, he knew, kept a large supply of reproduction knobbly walking sticks, doled out to visitors and, on one

occasion, it was rumoured, to his housekeeper, in lieu of a bonus. Kaye wound down the limo window and propelled the walking stick into the Lanarkshire countryside.

Even now, seven decades later, Scotland empathises. No single person did so much to inculcate and popularise the idea of Scottish meanness, to further the belief that Scots are penny-pinching, cheese-paring, miserly spendthrifts. Lauder it was who stood by as the metaphoric fingerless gloves were pulled over Caledonia's spindly, blue digits. In a thousand music-hall routines he poked gentle, but barbed, fun at the fiscal caution of the Scot. One routine described a Scot who, sold a sheet containing one thousand pins, counts them to discover there are only 998; the Scot who calls his mother to wish her happy birthday and reverses the charges; the Scot who when told a banana costs a penny asks if he can have three for tuppence.

How had Lauder, singer of 'Roamin' in the Gloaming' and 'Keep Right on to the End of the Road', come by the idea that Scots are fiercely cheapskate? Possibly he derived it from accounts of the early days of the Free Church in Scotland which, having no means of support, no backers and no property, was obliged, somewhat scandalously, to charge worshippers entrance to its Easter service. Perhaps Lord Byron made a contribution when he described Scotland as 'a land of meanness, sophistry and mist'. In his *Tour of the Western Isles* Dr Johnson was appalled to learn the islanders had no conventional currency. Legend has it Charles Dickens took the Christian name of his miser Ebeneezer Scrooge from a founder of the Church of Scotland. And once Lauder had kicked things off the theme was picked up enthusiastically by the likes of *Punch* magazine, always keen on a spot of cross-border mischief.

Whatever its origin the misconception is in place yet. We remember particularly the Scottish hotel guest in *Fawlty Towers*, locked in heated debate with Basil over some piffling extra on his bill: 'Tell you what,' says Fawlty, 'let's scratch that ten pence, live a little.' In one of his comic essays Woody Allen states that copper wire was invented by two Scotsmen fighting over a penny (though the origin of this quip may have been Jewish (as the century progressed Scottish and Jewish meanness became comedically interchangeable). Upon the Donald McGill seaside postcard of British identity the Lauder proposition is resplendent still, its Scotsmen in kilts and bunnets, red-nosed and Argyll-socked, complaining over the larcenous price of candy floss.

And then there are the verbal jokes, exchanged everyday in pubs and playgrounds and keeping the libel on life-support. Such as the one about the Scotsman who drops a fifty-pence piece, bends down to pick it up and feels it hit him on the back of the neck. Or the Scotsman who removes from his pint a drowning fly and instructs it to spit out what it had swallowed. Or the Scotsman so incensed by a newspaper's obsession with Scottish thrift he contacts the editor to warn that, should the comments persist, he will cease forthwith to borrow the paper in question.

It is true that this reputation for meanness still bemuses most Scots, as anyone who ever tried declining the offer of a drink at last orders will attest. Neither did Lauder reckon with the tradition of Highland hospitality, so vigorous even now that it all but obliges the provider to abase themselves through generosity. Lauder's stereotype, if he did exist, was a creature of a different age, one of stricter religious observance, of greater community nosiness, of lower wages and larger families. The Scot was hampered also by being identifiable, geographically and sartorially, more so than the average Geordie or Liverpudlian struggling to make ends meet. There was, it must be conceded, something innately comedic in the look and sound of the classic Highland Scot, so distinct from his trousered lowland brother. Add to this the music-hall appetite for novelty and oddity, for tribal solidarity, and Lauder's claims seem more explicable. The mean Scot was a character, a construct, as real as claims that Stan Laurel was a dim-wit.

There are signs that in later life Lauder thought better of his creation: 'I suppose we shall never get away from the taunt of meanness against Scotsmen,' he said in 1925. 'It is one of those jokes that have come to stay – like wireless and porridge. In the remote past someone made a joke at the expense of a cautious Scotsman, and that joke has spread all over the world and persisted to this day.

'I suppose that if at that time somebody had said an Englishman's chief characteristic was his meanness the joke would have had the same remarkable run and we should still be laughing at jokes about and Englishman and his money.' He didn't, however. Like the Scotsman trying to cash a Clydesdale Bank tenner in Surrey, the slur is merely something he has no option but to live with.

Neil Lennon

Those who doubt Neil Lennon's eligibility for an identity parade of shame and obloquy such as this are advised to view a piece of footage traceable readily on the internet. Shot on a mobile phone, it captures Lennon, manager of Celtic Football Club, in a lively setting; a pub or a social club. He is singing, after a fashion, in the lusty, variable manner of the comprehensively sozzled. The song is some piece of scatological doggerel pertaining to Rangers, Celtic's principal rivals. The opposing team, suggests Lennon, are little better than bodily waste, an opinion held in defiance of the fact that Rangers have long been the more successful side.

No matter. Clearly, the ditty is not intended as an inventory of title flags and cup wins, but, rather, is being sung to aggrandise carousing colleagues, in a spirit of ardent, doctrinaire aggression. This is the truly remarkable thing about it. Managers of football teams have since time immemorial been figures of fun, depicted archetypically as blokes in late middle age, garbed in sheepskin coats, struggling to convey the simplest concept without recourse to the mixed metaphor. He and his ilk were captured to perfection by Peter Cook in the character Alan Latchley, who opined that 'Football is about nothing unless it's about something – and what it's about is . . . football'. It would take some effort to picture, say, Bill Shankly or Sir Matt Busby in T-shirts, drunkenly berating the opposition in songs so puerile they'd embarrass a six-year- old. By tradition, football managers were dull and sober, dreary and diplomatic.

That, however, was prior to the advent of Neil Lennon. In his pomp, Lennon was perhaps the most combative and dismaying figure in the history of British sport. Football in the west of Scotland, of course, has always been a snake pit, a confined space in which the auld enemies of Rangers and Celtic have transacted their hissy, venomous battles for supremacy. Rangers win the league one year and Celtic win it the following year. Since the late 1800s this, more or less, has been the way of it. The model is Manichean and binary. No other team has ever had a look-in. Not for nothing are Rangers and Celtic known collectively as the Old Firm: theirs is a marriage, an alliance, a partnership in which, essentially, the frictions are perpetuated by fans only; by, if you will, the shareholders. At board level, meanwhile, a businesslike impassivity has prevailed. Glasgow has always had potential to be a powder keg, so grievous is its history of sectarian attrition, a conflict played out even more spectacularly still in Northern Ireland. Aware of this, the higher echelons of Rangers, as the Protestant side, and Celtic, as the Catholic, were obliged to play it cool, to mind their language, to forego the vigorously colourful squabbles that are part and parcel of footballing life.

And then, as we say, came Lennon. The Irishman did something truly, deeply regrettable. He breached the *cordon sanitaire*. He opened the can marked DO NOT OPEN and affected surprise when he found within it a good many oozy, slithery invertebrates. He broke the embargo, he spoke the forbidden word. He took umbrage at unfavourable decisions from referees and football authorities. He missed no opportunity to disclaim any belief in a conspiracy against Celtic, and thereby missed no opportunity to describe the frightful conspiracy that fortunately did not exist, like Mark Anthony praising Brutus at Caesar's funeral.

The arrant unlikelihood of all this became evident in the 2012/13 season, once Rangers had been demoted from the Scottish Premier League to Division Three of the Scottish Football League, on account of (later discredited) financial irregularities. Relieved of the need to compete against the sole Scottish team superior to his own, Lennon suddenly found himself in a sunnier mood. His gripes were consigned to history: no longer did Lennon claim habitually, as he'd done during seasons 2008 through 2010, that referees gave decisions and penalties against Celtic almost as a matter of course. No longer was Lennon quite so vexed by disobliging media coverage of Celtic, or by the Scottish Football Association when it penalised him for misbehaving during matches round the perimeter of the pitch. There was an end to the almost daily Lennon press conference jeremiad, full of insinuations and carefully phrased observations. There'd be no repeat of the incident following a Scottish Cup match at Celtic's ground, when a snarling Lennon needed to be held back from Ally McCoist, manager of Rangers. Without the necessity of keeping parity with Rangers, the stresses and tensions that had made Lennon so volatile seemed to vanish.

Despite all this, it remained possible to possess a measure of sympathy for Lennon. In 2008 he was set upon in the street by two Rangers fans; three years later the Royal Mail intercepted a parcel bomb addressed to him and later a supporter of Hearts FC was jailed for assaulting Lennon during a match. If anything, the attacks bore out the advisability of the approach Lennon had disregarded; it was for properly constructive reasons the owners of Rangers and Celtic pursued a see-no-evil, speak-no-evil policy. After ripping it up, Lennon may well have wished the genie back into the bottle.

There was also clearly a sense in which Lennon was over-invested in his mission. Most football managers are phlegmatic about the fortunes of the teams they marshal: they do their best and the better they do the more secure they make their own employment futures. Journeyman thinking of this kind does not cut it for Old Firm managers, however. The job is, by convention, a poisoned chalice. The rules are simple – win convincingly and constantly, or close the door on your way out. Such happened to the Celtic manager preceding Lennon, and his hasty exit necessitated giving the job to an untried aspirant. Many of Lennon's mistakes, then, we can put down to the zealousness of an ambitious man unable to land a glove on his greatest opponents. So we understand, we empathise. But also we are bound to note that, for several years at least, the sporting aspects and Queensbury rules of Scottish football were sadly somewhat diminished. Commentators tend to dub the sectarian friction between Rangers and Celtic as 'Scotland's secret shame'. Under Neil Lennon, this shame became rather less covert.

John Leslie

There are certain stories the British press adore, for bearing out so colourfully its argument that civilisation is going to hell in a hand cart. A classic of the genre involves those blokes working as department store Santas who get blind drunk on the job. Another is the rocketing price of strawberries at Wimbledon. Or coverage of men whose wives divorce them for their succumbing to some overmastering obsession, like filling the living room with a life-size replica of the Starship Enterprise ('It's a hobby, Jim, but not as we know it' went one headline). Each of these tales will provoke the necessary response: a sigh, a shake of the head, a belief that bit by bit the social and cultural verities are crumbling away to nothing.

But one variant dominates all others, is a Godzilla of the form: to wit, the shamed *Blue Peter* presenter. This story is the big one. A five-year-old child could see the scandalous paradox it contains, which is rather the nub of the story's singular power to outrage. You know *Blue Peter*, of course. Since the late 1950s the show was the BBC beacon that guided the children of Britain towards constructive activity and selfless endeavour. Twice a week, Mondays and Thursdays, it appeared, with its well-scrubbed presenters, its studio-bound pets and its To-Do list of improving tasks. John Noakes might be reporting from the summit of Nelson's Column, followed by a group of Methodist roller-skaters from Guernsey. Valerie Singleton might construct a Tardis from a tissue-box as Peter Purves interviewed David Essex. Long before Band Aid, *Blue Peter* was collecting milk-bottle tops for famine relief. The show inculcated in its viewers both curiosity and kindness and asked of them only that they stay insulated within its bubble of Corinthian diligence. It was bloody marvellous, *Blue Peter*, now we come to think of it. The show is produced still, apparently, shown on a cable channel, though God knows what tasks are set these days; how to design a facial piercing for your thirty-eight-year-old grandmother, presumably.

It is easy to see why the fourth estate kept its eye on *Blue Peter*. Any emblem of virtue so conspicuous was clearly a story in waiting, lest that virtue slip. On occasions the vigilance was vindicated. Presenter Peter Duncan was found to have made some soft-porn flicks earlier in his career. The background of Michael Sundin was just as murky. The wondrous Janet Ellis was subjected to a singularly spurious tabloid outrage when she fell pregnant out of wedlock. Each incident was grist to the rumour mill. All of it, however, was mere prologue to the exploits of John Leslie, the show's first Scottish front person, a smooth, even-featured charmer known best for curtailing a relationship with the actress Catherine Zeta-Jones.

The role of *Blue Peter* presenter resembles the American presidency. The designation is seldom surrendered fully. Once a *Blue Peter* presenter, always a *Blue Peter* presenter, certainly as far as the British public is concerned. So Leslie discovered in 2002, eight years after he left the show, when he found himself in some very sticky legal lather indeed. It stemmed back to an autobiography written recently by Ulrika Jonsson, the well-known television personality. Jonsson's book made a striking claim, that some years previously she had been raped by a colleague. Jonsson did not identify her attacker, and has never done so, but by whatever means the name of Leslie soon entered the frame.

At around the same time, an explicit home video Leslie had made two years earlier was leaked. It featured Leslie, an unidentified female friend and Leslie's then-partner Abi Titmuss, a tiny pneumatic nurse who later became a familiar face, and a familiar much else besides, in the world of adult entertainment. Her surname seemed further evidence that on this affair God was collaborating with a late scriptwriter of *Carry On* films. The video had the secondary effect of showing Leslie snorting cocaine, a predilection the *News of the World* rushed to expose on its front page. The presenter was relieved, if the term is to be used, of his duties presenting *This Morning*, a glossy magazine show on ITV. It was all some way from abseiling down Television Centre with a troop of Boy Scouts.

Titmuss was a constant presence when Leslie went to trial, click-clacking her way alongside her lofty and lugubrious swain. Police later dropped the charges against him, at which point Leslie appeared for the media, to claim he'd 'been to hell and back'. His luxurious spread in Barnes, London was sold. Leslie then embarked upon a decade of celebrity penance that he continues to pay. Titmuss too seemed to accept that the game was up and succumbed without shame to the blandishments of the world of soft-porn. Leslie split from her and returned to his home town of Edinburgh where he now operates, purportedly, as a property developer, one of the contexts in which his notoriety will count for little. He emerges but sporadically, to appear in low-budget pop videos or to submit to autopsy by star interviewer, wherein he concedes coyly that his manner of treating women had not always been what it should.

Although convicted of nothing, and with Ulrika Jonsson still declining to confirm who attacked her, Leslie's wholesale demise does at this distance seem a touch attritional. It takes effort to recall how seedy he seemed at the time. In particular, his timing was terrible. Years later the advent of *Big Brother, The Only Way Is Essex* and others would hint at the Roman excesses operating at the gaudier end of the show-business spectrum. In this context Leslie could have been something of a cult hero. However, he hailed from a daytime world of shiny suits and overstuffed sofas. Like the Bay City Rollers before him, Leslie found himself caught between two worlds, carrying the lowly into the rarefied realms of success and privilege. And, in the case of *Blue Peter*, of innocence. Those in television sometimes speak of the Curse of *Blue Peter*, the curious propensity the show had of attracting to its presenters varying degrees of misfortune. Nobody showed this curse in action quite like its first and to date only Scottish presenter.

Sir John Lockhart-Ross

The wilds of Scotland, from Inverness in the north to Loch Lomond near Glasgow, are sprinkled with statues, columns and cairns, each one commemorating the Highland Clearances. For objects that are dedicated to clearance they don't half clutter the place up. As recently as 2007, yet another was unveiled, in Helmsdale, Sutherland, entitled *Exiles*, a titanic hunk of kitsch depicting a bare-chested Highlander gazing with God-given forbearance into the middle-distance.

The Clearances are taken to have been, and still to be, a Very Bad Thing. Thousands of kilt-wearing, peat-cutting Highlanders were thrown off land upon which they eked their livings, merely in order that villainous lairds could lease it to sheep farmers. In effect, the Clearances made the Highlands one vast petting zoo. Swathes of remote, mountainous terrain were shorn of their meagre human settlement and given over to ovine chewers of the grass, a species seldom known to play bagpipes or to wrestle, in the accepted Highland fashion, with 18 lb babies, which only enhanced the bitterness of the process.

Duly, the serfs got the message and cleared off, mainly to North America, where with their unique combination of canniness and malevolence they prospered. Which raises a point. Where among these depictions of the Clearances, with their wretched, shawl-wrapped crofters hobbling towards passenger ships, is the memorial to what these people would become once they'd got to the other side? Where is the statue of, say, software tycoon Donald McLeod IV, with his Californian lingerie model wife and their four strapping, dentally impressive offspring? We await its construction.

Meanwhile, in certain parts of the Scottish interior, we need never wait long for conversation to turn to the Clearances. They are Scotland's Holocaust; a rupture the nation can never forget, along with all those other ruptures it can never forget like the Reformation, the Disruption or the 1978 World Cup. More critically, the Clearances are a lever, one of the mechanisms by which the Highlands levy guilt upon the lowlands. They are a still-weeping wound, and so much of what we know of Highland culture, from Gaelic to the tartanism of Sir Walter Scott, prospered on the basis that Highlanders had already suffered enough.

The presumption tends to be that the Clearances were initiated by titled English estate owners, leaping off their liveried horses to twist their wax moustaches and point sobbing Highlanders towards the nearest blizzard. This isn't strictly accurate. The man to whom the Clearances should be attributed is Sir John Lockhart-Ross, a prosperous soldier turned MP from Lanarkshire. He was the first estate owner to glance at a grazing black-face and sense a lightbulb activate above his head. Of course, history is seldom so causal. Much went on before Ross would nail his first eviction notice to his first barn door. MacLeod, the chief of clan MacLeod, had already attempted a spot of rationalisation on his estates on Skye. Macleod of Dunvegan and MacDonald of Sleat had tried selling plaid-clad crofters from their estates into slavery in the Carolinas.

Neither plan, however, had addressed satisfactorily the ongoing problem presented by the unity of the clans. Something more deci-sive was called for. The Union of the Crowns in 1707 had been a watershed moment, an attempt to put the British Isles into some kind of administrative order. That effort was confounded, though, by the reality that tribes of intractable men in skirts were wander-ing the Highlands, claiming loyalty to deposed king James Stewart. From Westminster and Whitehall word went out that the clans were to have their style cramped. Sundry restrictions on everyday life were stepped up. A Disarming Act and a Clan Act were brought in. The army stationed itself nearby in Fort William and Fort Augustus, just in case.

But the real pint-spilling, girlfriend-insulting, jacket-holding flare-up came in 1745 with the landing at Eriskay of Charles Edward Stuart, or Bonnie Prince Charlie, son of the miffed ex-monarch in question. By any standard his arrival meant the gloves were off. The resulting straightener, on the moors of Culloden, settled the matter decisively. The clans were routed and in the years that followed defeated Jacobites were taken to London to be tried for high treason; 120 were executed. Clan chiefs were denied rights to have grievances heard in court. Highland dress was banned by Act of Parliament. Jacobite supporters had their estates taken from them and given to factors. The clans were rendered as powerful as a gathering of Rotarians.

Thus was the stage set for the Clearances. Enter Sir John Lockhart-Ross. He was a standard-issue Scottish Hanoverian toff; navy officer and Member of Parliament for the constituency of Tain Burghs, a responsibility he discharged as grudgingly as he could, though he did rouse himself in 1796 to vote against the abolition of slavery. Ross dedicated himself to managing his estates, in which his reputation was impressive. In order to secure greater acreage, in Balnagowan in Cromarty, belonging formerly to a late relative, he adopted the name Ross. This was the turning point. After introducing to the Balnagowan estate in 1762 a sheep breed well-known in the Lowlands, the black-faced Linton, Lockhart-Ross granted a lease to a southern grazier, Thomas Geddes. By 1790, the Cheviot sheep had made its way into the County of Ross. The displacement of Highland families gained in momentum. The palsied Highland clan chiefs looked on dispassionately. Sheep farmers in the south got wind of developments and the Highland Clearance stepped up a gear.

The authorised version of proceedings has proved persistent, however. You gain a sense of its tenacity when visiting the Lios Mor, a whisky bar in Glasgow, much in thrall decoratively to the spirit of the '45. The urinals in the gents have inlaid into them the names of three English factors taken to have been instrumental in commissioning the Clearances. A sign invites drinkers to pay the men 'the tribute they are due'. The bar's stained glass window, meanwhile, shows the usual tableaux of crofter woe, with a family huddling on a quayside, preparing to depart their native land. Close inspection reveals the boat they will board is the *Waverley*, the paddle steamer that took generations of Glaswegians on bank holiday day-trips. The boat was built 200 years after the last cleared Highlander left the last croft.

Lulu

All things considered, it was serendipitous that Lulu's first hit single was entitled 'Shout!' The word can be adapted endlessly for newspaper headlines, as it has been in Lulu's case for five decades now. She is the 'Shout!' girl and rarely anything but. The avid reader of red-top tabloids can rest assured, then, that should Lulu have new information to impart it will without fail run beneath a headline declaring *Something To Shout About!* (translation: Lulu has a new album/has announced a tour). Or perhaps *Lulu's In With A Shout!* (translation: Lulu has entered the Eurovision Song Contest again). The variations have yet to be exhausted. We await patiently her collaboration with author Wilbur Smith on a project based round his bestselling war novel *Shout At the Devil*.

Such comments may be snarky but they contain a greater truth, namely that Lulu has been very visible for a very long time on the basis of some less than compelling contributions to the culture. Besides that 1963 debut, admittedly a bracing number with real personality, just as it had been when The Isley Brothers recorded it previously, the singer has struggled to make any kind of impact beyond existing as a kind of light entertainment Zelig: always turning up, always waving at the camera, always smiling, always answering, 'I'm very glad you asked me that, Richard'.

She began her career as a credible, if unseasoned, pop-blues vocalist, rather in the style of Cilla Black or Dusty Springfield. She has ended up flogging jewellery on satellite shopping channels. In between she donned whatever motley was tossed at her: actress (in the 1967 classroom romance *To Sir, With Love*); singer of a James Bond theme (*The Man With The Golden Gun*, 1974); paramour of David Bowie, Bee Gee Maurice Gibb and of celebrity hairdresser John Frida; purveyor of cougar sex-gran chic courtesy of a late-career collaboration with Take That; not to mention sundry spells in panto, traditionally last resort of the pathologically attention-bent.

More difficult to find, though, is any evidence of a successful and sustained career as a singer of any repute. In 2002 she published *I Don't Want To Fight*, her autobiography, or rather her second autobiography, Lulu having already produced one in 1986. Writing an autobiography is one of the classic, time-killing strategies of the underemployed but mildly renowned, allowing them the sizzle of publicity as it denies them the meat of real achievement. The endpapers of *I Don't Want To Fight* told the whole story, being a display of Lulu record sleeves down the years. It was a terrifying array. Bubble-perms and denim jackets with the collars turned up vied for space with jump suits, sailor outfits and demi-waves of quite ferocious rigour. Every ill-advised style of the previous forty years was collected together. It resembled an Oxfam bargain bin preserved between hard covers. Her career was always a curious and wayward one, quite distinct from those of peers like Marianne Faithfull or Sandie Shaw. Those girls could trade on their presence at the epicentre of the swinging vortex. They had credibility that in time has become iconic. Lulu was within spitting distance of the same vortex – Jimi Hendrix famously had the plugs pulled while appearing on her BBC show *Happening for Lulu* in 1969 – but she was always a different proposition, immeasurably more malleable and timid.

Or, perhaps, just canny. As late as the mid-1960s, those who ran the British entertainment industry presumed pop music was just a flash in the pan. Certainly this was the thinking of Lulu's then manager, Marian Massey, who wanted for her client a proper career rather than a clutch of soon-forgotten hits. And so Lulu appeared in her first pantomime, *Peter Pan*, in 1966. She has been an all-round entertainer ever since – never hip, just the Glasgow lass who parlayed 'Shout!' into a four-decade marathon of can-dance, can-sing froth. 'Given my time again,' she told me, thoughtfully, 'I'd rather have been Joni Mitchell than Sammy Davis Jr.'

The other great inhibiting factor in Lulu's life was her parents, Eddie and Betty Lawrie. Even at the height of her fame, the wraith of their protection pursued her. The hard-forged and humble values of Glasgow's east end bristled when faced with the louche standards of showbiz. Anticipating her parents' disapproval was what kept the young star in check. 'Kenny Everett made fun of the fact,' she wrote in her autobiography, 'that I was the one cleaning ashtrays and making tea while everyone else was stoned.' Her memoir contains a number of such vignettes: the nervous outsider, the innocent abroad. 'Don't marry a wee man, Marie,' her mother told her when she started dating Davy Jones of The Monkees. 'They all have Napoleon complexes.'

It wasn't, she has admitted, as though her parents were paragons themselves. Her father, an offal dresser at the Gallowgate meat market, was a rollicking alcoholic who beat his wife as the children cowered under the bed. Her mother was desperately needy and developed what the singer has termed an 'obsession' with her. She went from cosseted child star – Lulu was fifteen when 'Shout!' was released – to doting wife with no meaningful intermediate stage. Today she is a meditating, macrobiotic mid-life survivor, much given to Oprah-esque, go-girlfriend phraseology, the stuff that's now a *lingua franca* for impressionable celebrities. She talks, *ad nauseum* it must be said, about the power of positive thinking and of living in the moment. And then, famously, there are her looks, or rather their preservation. They are what Lulu is renowned most for these days: looking better than she did forty years ago. 'That's the question I'm asked most often now,' she has said. 'What's your secret?' Of course the secret, as it is for most ageing celebrities, is good lighting, in tandem with a comfortable lifestyle. The mediated Lulu looks like a poster girl for HRT, shiny and soft-focused. In the flesh, though, time's depredations of time are rather more conspicuous. Her skin has a bumpy, pouched quality and only surgery could conceal a sixty-four-year-old neck. This not to be cruel or boorish, merely to point out that some manner of swizz is being transacted.

None of the above, however, not Lulu's creative shortcomings nor her family background, tell the whole tale as to why Lulu is so derided in modern Scotland, why she has come to be held in such low regard, why she does not feature proudly or prominently in the family photo Scotland keeps on the baronial mantelpiece. The reason is simple and oddly counter-intuitive. It's that Lulu doesn't talk proper; or, rather, because she fails to speak in the voice in which Scotland would have her speak. She speaks in the voice you would expect her to, that of someone who moved from Glasgow in her teens to a world of Thames Valley, two-car-garage social climbers. Her tones are rounded and well-modulated. But she can 'speak' Glaswegian when she wishes to, and does so; to oblige demands from local media during visits back to Glasgow and so on. No doubt, say, Britt Ekland and Ulrika Jonsson can drop into fluent Swedish dialect when occasion demands. Neither, however,

ever did so with the coy, winsome, disingenuously punchable smugness of Lulu. To watch her slip into Glaswegian drag is a profoundly horrible experience, a betrayal of both what she once was and what she later became. We witnessed something similar when around 2000 Madonna began transacting her love affair with London: again we sensed that familiar nimbus of verbal *eau de cologne*,that same furrowed concentration.

Lulu, however, was the progenitor, the original who was never equalled. Prior to Lulu the wider British audience had never heard a young, with-it Scottish Glaswegian accent. It was a state of affairs Lulu took pains to leave unaltered. Scotland has never quite forgiven her. The nation's place at the Longest Cocktail Party was assumed by some interloper, a turncoat, who turned her origins into a party piece.

Gordon Matheson

The city of Glasgow is an untypical place, more a city-state than anything. The locals are quite proud of this. By tradition, they feel scant fraternity with the remainder of Scotland. Edinburgh, they maintain, is merely twee, pretty and old-fashioned; a page in the *Rough Guide* and not much beside. Aberdeen is wreathed in mist and smells of mackerel. Dundee is a broken and bestial place. Other settlements are just sources of mirth: Perth and Stirling, with their snoozy swathes of farmland; Inverness, slumbering quietly in the 1940s. And don't even mention Shetland, Orkney or the western isles, those havens of Satanic abuse, agricultural necromancy and folk music. Rather, the Glaswegian finds his kinfolk to the west, in Ireland and America. The Glaswegian experience, feels the native, is bracingly, unapologetically urban, cosmopolitan and egalitarian.

All the above has bred a certain independence in Glasgow's civic soul, expressed particularly in its city council. In most cities, these bodies are fairly anonymous, arbiters of licensing hours and the frequency of bin collection. But not in Glasgow. Here, the city council is the beating heart of local life, almost a kind of secular Vatican or like something from Kafka's novel *The Castle*, extending its tendrils into each nook of everyday activity. It is a council with personality, ineradicably socialist in character, a proactive partner in the ongoing project of what it means to be Glaswegian.

One example was seen in the 1980s when Glasgow was at its lowest ebb, considered widely a problem city, riven with social decay and street violence. Glasgow retaliated with a PR campaign that had a bright yellow Mr Man as its mascot; Mr Happy, as it happened. The Glasgow's Miles Better campaign was bizarre and lateral but it worked. Glasgow undertook a gradual journey from hellhole to hotspot, lauded for its stone-cleaned Victorian architecture and its credo of can-do.

No doubt memories of the campaign were in mind when in 2011 the council turned its attentions to George Square. The square is Glasgow's front garden, a football-pitch sized space in the heart of the city, sitting on the doorstep of City Chambers, headquarters of the council. Together, chambers and square represent a kind of omphalos in the city, a place of temporal and recreational focus.

Yet a problem developed. Since the 1960s the square had become contested ground. Formerly it was a pleasing and classic arrangement of statues, benches, shrubs and flowers, laid out to maximise both form and function. Over the years, though, successive administrations had tried to leave their mark. On a regular basis the square was shuffled and reordered, to the point where it relinquished both appeal and utility. George Square was more a battle-ground, on which architects town planners doodled whatever design whims were prevailing that year. This culminated, disastrously, with the square being overlaid with a carpet of bright red tarmac. This lent it the aesthetic appeal and civic grandeur of a municipal lorry park.

Something had to be done, and this is where the problems began. Enter one Gordon Matheson. Elected Lord Provost in May 2010, Matheson, a cheerful, chubby fellow whose natty spectacle frames and well-cut pinstripe suits set him apart from his dowdier colleagues, was judged to have made a good fist as Grand Pooh-bah of the council. He had fought off a challenge for the seat from the SNP. He was named local politician of the year. He was liked and respected, particularly for stepping up when his predecessor, Stephen Purcell, suffered a breakdown that exposed relationships with suspected criminals and cocaine use. Matheson was considered a safe and competent pair of hands.

And then one day he glanced out his office window, noticed George Square was looking scruffy and thus set in train the debacle that would effectively end his political career, all for the sake of a few wilting oak trees. For Matheson had had a lightbulb moment, involving a wholesale redesign of the square, soup to nuts, top to bottom. The idea betrayed total misunderstanding of Glasgow's citizenry, who liked the square the way it was but wished it wasn't the colour of a clown's bow-tie.

Matheson pressed on anyway, inviting from architectural consultancies around the globe proposals for a new, improved George Square. Duly, the schemes were submitted. They were radical and radically rubbish. One proposed converting the square into what seemed a giant reflective paddling pool. Another did away with the red tarmac but replaced it with a forest of spouting water features. Another, Matheson's personal favourite, featured more spouting water, a marble expanse and a weird stone arch. The redesign was budgeted at £15m.

Glasgow was scandalised. Awoken was the kraken that sleeps in its soul, roused only by bureaucratic bumbling of quite egregious magnitude. A protest group was founded and made welcome on every media outlet in the area. Rallies were held. The George Square protest was perhaps the biggest outbreak of civic disgruntlement seen in the city since opposition to the poll tax twenty years earlier. The council voted and opted for a design other than Matheson's favourite. Immediately, the council leader declared the revamp would be cancelled and replaced by a modest facelift. Reporting on the shambles, the Royal Incorporation of Architects in Scotland concluded: 'From his initial comments at the first judges' meeting onwards, it appears that, for whatever reason, Councillor Matheson had selected his own winner at the outset and reasoning by a very experienced group of judges did not persuade him otherwise.'

Although the RIAS's complaint to the Commissioner of Ethical Standards in Public Life ended with him being cleared of any improper conduct, Matheson's behaviour was a wondrous display of petulance, redolent of another age, when the council cardinals treated the city as their personal fiefdoms. Certainly the affair has probably done for Matheson whose ambition to run for parliament in 2016 is now thought to be holed below the waterline; victim of hubris and of the ancient, elemental wrath of the city he ran.

Kenny MacAskill

ike children peering through the window of a public house, Scottish politicians ache to fraternise with the grown-ups; to strut, fret and swank upon an international stage. One thing has always impeded this: Westminster. Tradition has determined that the wallahs down south do all the heavy lifting, the treaties and trade agreements, the economic summits, while their counterparts in Scotland are merely a janitoriat, handling local hospitals and education. Long term, this is not good for the soul. Deep in the Scottish nationalist psychology a tiny voice mutters darkly, cursing its luck, hoping against hope for a chance to shine, complaining that it's bloody Norway and Iceland who get all the weekend mini-breaks to Washington.

So intense is this longing it comes to border on reverie. A lone bagpipe skirls in the Highland distance as visions swim before the eyes. Nicola Sturgeon and the Secretary of State are deep in discussion while scrutinising a sheet of statistics. On the White House lawn, Mike Russell laughs ruefully as another baseball eludes his bat. Kevin Spacey nods as Alex outlines the restoration of the Forth and Clyde Canal. This is how it could be. Instead, Salmond spends his week in the Scottish parliament fending off hordes of opponents, like a chubby Bruce Lee. Remote remains the hope of any meaningful engagement with the wider world, so long as Westminster is ahead in the queue.

Seeds of change were sown on 21 December 1988, when Pan Am flight 103, London to New York, exploded in the skies over Lockerbie, killing 270. The consequent quest for justice saw, as Scotland's Lord Advocate pointed out, the UK's largest criminal inquiry being led by its smallest police force, Dumfries and Galloway Constabulary. Following a joint investigation by the force and the FBI, a suspect was identified, Abdelbaset al-Megrahi, an officer in the Libyan secret service, operating on the orders of president Muammar Gaddafi. In 2001 al-Megrahi was convicted and installed in Greenock Prison. He had served eight years when he was diagnosed with prostate cancer. Doctors gave him three months to live.

It was at this point that up stepped Kenny MacAskill, minister for justice in the Scottish government and therefore, with justice being a devolved matter, the man with the decision. MacAskill had never made much of a splash previously, coming across as a rather grey figure, a technocrat, devoted to the party line and to pleasing his leader. He had the bearing of a grammar school know-it-all, a founder of societies and sports clubs. Indeed, his feeling for the Scotland football team was so lively that in 1999 he was arrested on suspicion of drunkenness as he made his way to a Euro 2000 qualifier against England at Wembley.

MacAskill moved centre stage again with the al-Megrahi diagnosis. A majority of victims aboard flight 103 had been American and this had lent a certain vigour to the attitude of the families who survived them. The evidence against al-Megrahi may have been debated hotly but consensus held that the proper perpetrator was being punished, a state of affairs the families were resistant to seeing amended. MacAskill and the Scottish government felt differently. In 2009 it was announced that al-Megrahi would be released on compassionate grounds and returned to Tripoli to die in the bosom of his family. MacAskill claimed he was 'bound by Scottish values to release him'. The decision provoked international outrage. Glenn Johnson, whose daughter Beth Ann was returning home for Christmas when she died, caught the mood in asking: 'How can a person who killed 270 people, who had no compassion for them, be given compassion? It is another tragedy families have to suffer.' This response was typical. President Obama described the decision as 'a mistake'. Again and again, Americans expressed their disgust, their heartbreak, their wholesale bewilderment.

Scots were bewildered too, for different reasons. Admittedly, they weren't so invested in al-Megrahi being the bad guy, not quite so scandalised by his handover to Libya. But something rankled. Repeatedly, Salmond and MacAskill justified their decision on the grounds of the ancient and venerable traditions of Scottish compassion. It was almost as though a wizard's spell were being invoked; as if compassion was a component of Scottish chromosomes, along with the gene for ginger hair. This predilection came as news to most Scots, few of whom seemed aware that in the compassion lottery they, as Scots, held the winning ticket. There was some tradition in it, admittedly. Scottish judicial compassion was held to be self-evident and inalienable, a brand almost, like German efficiency or Italian flair. The SNP government appeared to derive a measure of gratification from the unpopularity of its actions, as though the taking of tough decisions were a hallmark of government. The point was underlined by the *Chicago Tribune* when it wrote of 'MacAskill's self-praising paean to his own mercy'.

Public opinion held that a dubious decision had been reached by a curiously antagonistic process. MacAskill and his party seemed to be flying wilfully in the face of global opinion, for the sake of a virtue that hadn't been emphasised so stridently before. There was a deluge of polls: the *Daily Mail* found 51 per cent of Scots opposing the decision, with 43 per cent in support; the BBC found 60 per cent opposition; *The Times* put wider British opposition at 61 per cent, with 45 per cent adamant that al-Megrahi's release had less to do with compassion than with ensuring Scotland favourable terms in any future oil negotiations. MORI put the reckoning at 47 per cent against, with 40 per cent in support. An ICM poll showed 74 per cent believing the affair had damaged Scotland's reputation. Former Labour MP and Scottish Office minister Brian Wilson wrote that the decision 'shamed' Scotland. America was hardly inclined to disagree. Secretary of State Hillary Clinton called the decision 'absolutely wrong'. The *New York Times* wrote that 'for many Americans, his release rekindled the agony and anguish of loss and provoked questions about the notions of compassion and justice used by Scotland to justify its decision'. In an open letter to MacAskill, FBI director Robert Mueller, lead investigator in the bombing, said he was 'outraged at the decision, blithely defended on the grounds of "compassion"'. An internet campaign, Boycott Scotland, was founded, urging the avoidance of Scottish exports and visits.

Further chickens roosted in August 2009 when al-Megrahi was flown into Tripoli, where in celebration the waiting crowds waved Saltires. The gesture was as provocative and mordant as anything in the events preceding it. The handling of al-Megrahi had been posited upon a life expectancy of three months; embarrassingly for MacAskill he went on to live for three years. Now, nearly five years on, tourism to Scotland from North America has yet to recover to pre-Megrahi levels. American senators and diplomats have declined repeatedly to take any position on Scottish independence. The bad taste MacAskill left in the world's mouth has yet to dispel completely; this after a spell in the global limelight soured by incompetence, controversy, conspiracy theory, bad faith and poor judgement. And further proof of the truism, that we should be careful what we wish for.

Ally MacLeod

Little summarises the narrative of modern Scotland, the way an innate sense of superiority and destiny can be contradicted consistently by blunt empirical fact, quite like the 1978 World Cup in Argentina. Almost four decades on, the tournament remains the nightmare from which Scotland can never wake; the car crash that in the national psyche plays on endless loop. Scots talk of a national talent for plucking defeat from the jaws of victory. Give a Scot an open goal, says the truism, and he will launch the ball way beyond the stands, possibly into the greenhouse of a blameless pensioner. The assumption is fatalistic, mordant and depressive; a self-fulfilling prophecy. It came true never more conspicuously than at the finals of the 1978 World Cup, where for Scotland open goals and the avoidance of same became horribly actual.

On this occasion, though, there was a twist. Defeat was snatched not from the jaws of victory but from a mirage. Even the tiniest prospect of victory, or even of dignity, had been illusory, a phantom; but one seen and described in heartless detail by Ally MacLeod, manager of the national squad. An amiable and enthusiastic man, his sizeable conk and weak chin giving him semblance to a heron in a tracksuit, MacLeod has gone into history as perhaps the most energetic fantasist, the most garrulous fabulist sport ever produced; a man who by comparison made Muhammad Ali look cautious, bashful and tentative.

MacLeod's fervour that summer does need to be seen in context, though. At the time a restive air surrounded the Scottish national team. Long had it been considered a crew of middling journeymen, unremarkably unspectacular. But a new era seemed to be appearing on the horizon. The oddly charismatic MacLeod, determined but inherently comic, an unblinking waffler, was appointed Scotland supremo following a respectable career managing Ayr and Aberdeen. 'My name is Ally MacLeod,' he'd said in introduction to his Scotland squad, 'and I am a winner.' Dame Reality considered this claim and shrugged half-heartedly. Initially, MacLeod acquitted himself well, by securing his team's passage to Argentina, a feat made all the sweeter by the corresponding failure of Scotland's deadliest enemy, England. Further confidence came in the commonly held opinion that MacLeod had taken charge of a Scotland squad of untypically high calibre, including Joe Jordan, Kenny Dalglish and Willie Johnson. The team, MacLeod believed, and stated repeatedly to all who'd listen, stood an excellent chance of winning the World Cup, or returning with 'at least a medal'. Unaccustomed to such brazen boosterism and with its critical faculties duly bamboozled, the nation took MacLeod at his word. Gradually, the claim came to feel less preposterous. As the finals approached apprehension was replaced by anticipation. For once in Scotland's history the clouds were parting and the sun glinting through. Andy Cameron, a popular comedian, released the tub-thumping anthem 'Ally's Tartan Army' ('We're gonna shake them up/When we lift the World Cup,' went the lyrics). The single reached No 6 in the charts and earned Cameron an appearance on *Top of the Pops*. MacLeod and the team appeared on television nightly, advertising carpets. A giddy, insistent hysteria took hold, whipped up by the manager and his nerveless rhetoric. Twenty-five thousand fans turned up at Hampden Park to bid the team *bon voyage*. At Prestwick Airport MacLeod was asked what he planned to do after the World Cup. With what had become his trademark blend of defiant levity, he answered: 'Retain it.'

Did Scotland truly believe MacLeod would come good? That his team of competent but middling hoofers would stroll past Brazil and Italy and West Germany? Bizarrely, it did. The entire nation embarked upon a sabbatical from reason. The period leading up to the team's opening match felt, quite literally, like a carnival, a farewell to the flesh, an away-day from common sense. MacLeod became a proselytizer, winning souls over to his credo of can-do. In time, of course, the folly of such thinking would become apparent. Until then, Scotland would howl in the moonlight and bathe in the morning dew, dizzy with willing suspension of disbelief.

The nation, however, could not see behind the scenes. In the team's Cordoba headquarters the gilt was coming away from the gingerbread. In-fighting broke out between players over the generosity, or otherwise, of bonus packages offered for victories. Midfielder Willie Johnson was sent home in disgrace when a cold remedy he'd been taking turned out to contain a banned substance. A row developed over the team being sponsored by the British American Tobacco Company. Dr David Player of the Scottish Health Education Unit Health asked that Scotland withdraw from the deal. MacLeod refused, in his blithe, inimitable way: 'I told him several of our players smoke and it would be untruthful to back an anti-smoking campaign.'

The inevitable came to pass. Hubris and insufficient preparation conspired to confound. Scotland lost its opening game, with Peru, 3-1. Its next, with Iran, should have been a stroll in the park but

MacLeod's team scraped only a 1-1 draw and that thanks to an Iranian own goal. The next match, against Holland, was more agonising yet. Holland were among the most feared teams in the tournament and, indeed, went on to be its runner-up. Common sense dictated that Scotland would receive a pasting. Bizarrely, they emerged triumphant, winning 3-2, even scoring the Goal of the Tournament thanks to a flash of mazy wizardry from Archie Gemmell. In any other circumstance this would have been a glorious victory, a real slice of giant-killing. In the actual circumstances, the win was merely sickening, the very definition of too little too late, rendered all the more bitter when Scotland failed to progress to the next round, thwarted by goal difference rather than points tally. In essence the dream had died for the sake of a single goal, conceded against vastly inferior opposition. A fate more vexing and nullifying, more exquisitely cruel, could not have been designed by a sadist with time on their hands.

MacLeod and his team came home in the lowest of dudgeons, to be welcomed by the lamentations of the nation as it blinked in the cold morning light. MacLeod would spend the next thirty years atoning, turning up on the sofas of television chat shows and in the press to get his wrists slapped. He became the nation's holy fool, its disgraced uncle, though the recriminations were usually played for laughs. It was to Scotland's credit, one supposes, that few bore MacLeod any lasting ill will. The damage was too deep, too traumatic to be accessed readily. Again, it must be stressed that for Scotland the World Cup of 1978 was not merely a football competition ahead of which the nation allowed its expectations to get out of hand, rather as England has done ahead at every World Cup since 1966. Rather, the Argentina campaign was an almost-religious event, a crusade, a mass hysteria; weirdly enjoyable yet utterly spurious; the closest sport has come to pantomime. If nothing else, then, Ally MacLeod made a decent Pied Piper, conjuring from his flute tunes that were unexpectedly bewitching but that led Scotland to a mystic realm only he could see.

Frank McAveety

We all know the type – the bloke with the distended midriff of middle age, bulbous beneath the crumpled T-shirt upon which is emblazoned the name of his favourite band: The Who, AC/DC, Led Zeppelin; even, saints preserve us, Lynyrd Skynyrd. Nothing says *reluctantly adult* quite like a never-dwindling passion for rock music.

For rock is the training bra of musical appreciation, a taste from which some are never weaned. And this can become problematic, because rock is associated inextricably with the vigour and passion of youth: Mick Jagger doing his funky chicken dance for 50,000 Californian space cadets; Jimi Hendrix setting fire sullenly to his Fender Stratocaster. Rock is the childish thing many choose never to put away. Which is fine for as long as the fan remains as sappy and callow as the genre itself. Gradually, however, the years pass. The girth thickens. The temples grey. Their homes come to require upkeep, a process invigilated by partners who can live quite happily without their fifty-year-old husbands mimicking yet again the guitar solo from 'Bohemian Rhapsody'.

We see his type everywhere: in bars, feeding the jukebox; in newsagents, perusing the range of glossy magazines produced for his gouty gratification; or in the few record shops that remain. As he flicks through the racks he will habitually toss back the hair he no longer has and, if moved by a particularly scorching riff coming through the speakers, will execute the Rock Overbite, a display in which the top row of teeth is placed over the bottom lip and the head nodded to indicate maximum vibe appreciation.

So, it is perfectly customary to spot these blokes in their natural habitats. You wouldn't imagine one of them to be the debating chamber of an elected parliament. But this would be to reckon without Frank McAveety, erstwhile MSP for Glasgow Shettleston. In his time, McAveety was perhaps the most laddish parliamentarian in British political history. The man had the gravitas of a roadie on rollerskates. He was dubbed the Minister for Photo Opportunities. Calamity stalked him. In 2004 he got into an altercation with two anti-war protestors who, he claimed, subjected him to the worst intimidation he'd ever experienced. McAveety took the matter to court, though the sheriff noted he must have led a sheltered life and told him he had 'completely blown his credibility'. Then there was Piegate, when McAveety was forced to apologise for misleading parliament. He had missed the start of ministerial questions not, as he claimed, because he'd been detained on ministerial business but because he had been in the parliament canteen finishing his lunch. Later, he resigned from the parliament's Public Petitions Committee for making lascivious remarks about a woman in the public gallery, overheard because McAveety had neglected to remove his microphone.

All this would be dismaying at any time, but doubly so when McAveety was representing Shettleston, a constituency with pressing problems, particularly a quite abysmal health record. In Shettleston, male life expectancy is sixty-three, a figure beaten only by Burma, Nepal and Somalia. This might engender in a politician a certain soberness of bearing. But not necessarily in McAveety, whose tenure was a cavalcade of larky japes and hard-core album appreciation.

Perhaps this is a touch unfair; McAveety's career wasn't entirely cake and lemonade. He did have his uses. He served for two years as leader of Glasgow City Council, overseeing good works in the development of secondary schools and in securing debt relief for many in public housing. He campaigned successfully to bring sports infrastructure to the east end of Glasgow. He was in at the birth of the Standards Commission for Scotland, which seemingly was quite a good thing.

It isn't wholly fanciful, though, to imagine that while McAveety was doing all this he had a sneaky copy of *New Musical Express* secreted on his lap or the latest issue of *Mojo* hidden beneath his order papers. He could never quite shed his aura of overgrown schoolboy, or of enthusiastic partaker. He sat among a cast of colourful characters on the Left in Scotland, principally George Galloway and Tommy Sheridan, each of whom appeared also to believe that nothing was too good for the working class. Like that pair, McAveety came across as a law unto himself, a civic politician who had lucked his way into the big time and was seeking henceforth to ally good works with good times. For someone so keen on popular music, McAveety wasn't half prone to the off-key, to the bum note.

Exhibit one: his regular column in *Holyrood* magazine. Covering the policies and personalities of the Scottish parliament, this publication, usually, is middle-brow and worthy. Sample headline: Study Calls for New Entrepreneurial Approach in Not-for-Profit Housing. Aware, perhaps, that their pages could stand some enlivening, the editors introduced in 2004 a column entitled 'Frank McAveety's Classic Albums'. No longer was Frank's passion for the canon of classic rock to be shared with parliamentarians only; now the general public could experience what it might be like to be stuck next to Frank in a bus shelter or on a long train journey. The idea was radical. Never, for instance, had the *Spectator* run columns by the attorney-general discussing his favourite sitcoms. If Gordon Brown ever harboured a fondness for cartoon strips it went unmentioned in *Hansard*. No, only at Holyrood, with its open-necked, student union informality, could a senior politician write in the house journal about rock music yet escape being chased through the streets.

This was handy because McAveety had so much to tell us. To begin with, there was the scale of his album collection: 10,000 records, filed in alphabetical order and never lent out, after some unhappy experiences, he wrote. McAveety's taste was for the mainstream of rock music, the canon that ran from Presley to Radiohead. Particular fondness was reserved for the straining, gurning rock of Bruce Springsteen and for Van Morrison, particularly the live album *Too Late To Stop Now*, and for *Unknown Pleasures* by Joy Division, a band who named themselves after the prostitutes who serviced Nazi generals.

Of the former, the 'intensity of Van's vocals compels you as he builds up to an awesome scream, with the brass section blasting out behind him'. Barely pausing to scribble some graffiti on his school jotter, Frank went on to reveal that the 'much-neglected 'Wild Children' is taken to new heights by muted jazz trumpet and Spanish guitar' and that 'Listen to the Lion' 'implores, pleads, urges, slurs, scats, growls and snarls to its exhaustive conclusion [resulting] in an exclamatory "Alright" from an audience member.' One of McAveety's favourite Joy Division tracks, meanwhile, includes a lyric lamenting the object of desire's indifference to Ian Curtis' efforts to connect with her.

Honestly, Frank, could you blame us?

Hugh MacDiarmid

Those familiar with the BBC series *Monty Python's Flying Circus* will recall Ewan McTeagle, a recurring target of the show's Oxbridge absurdism. McTeagle was a poet; a tiny, kilted, muttering Central Casting Scotsman who dedicated his verses to the task of persuading acquaintances to lend him trifling sums of money. Across hill and glen McTeagle, with knobbly stick, would stride, composing aloud his stirring pleas for financial intercession.

It is difficult to be certain which Scottish poet the Python team was satirising. Clearly there was a touch of William McGonagall, the so-called worst poet ever, the man who on describing a railway disaster penned the lines: 'Beautiful railway bridge of the silv'ry Tay/Alas! I am very sorry to say/ That ninety lives have been taken away/On the last sabbath day of 1879/Which shall be remembered for a very long time.'

Present too is Sir Harry Lauder, who did so much to popularise the idea that Scots are financially careful to the point of mania. McTeagle's air of dreadful desperation had antecedents also in characters from Burns, Louis Stevenson and Sir Walter Scott, to say nothing of Private Fraser in *Dad's Army*, with his trademark cry of 'We're doomed!'

One candidate stands out, however, and this is Hugh MacDiarmid, author of 'A Drunk Man Looks at a Thistle'.

MacDiarmid is regarded widely, even since his death in 1978, as personification of the miserable, chippy, grumbling, resentful and torn-faced Scottish nightmare. The tendencies were inscribed into his face, an unsmiling, unblinking mask of disgruntled watchfulness, framed by a ski slope quiff of stiff white hair.

MacDiarmid was a formidably unpleasant individual, co-founder in 1928 of the SNP, later the author of *Plea for A Scottish Fascism* and thereby one who shared with Lord Reith the kind of Scottish temperament so stony it would embrace the advent of European totalitarianism. George Orwell included MacDiarmid on a list of political malcontents he compiled in 1949 for the British intelligence services. He was a plagiarist too, devising a poetic approach which defined, conveniently, prose written by others as poetry once it had been transplanted into poems MacDiarmid had written.

But it is his bearing for which we remember MacDiarmid most, for his haughty, dismissive impatience for anything insufficiently extreme or committed to the glorious project of Scottish identity. In *Who's Who* he listed his hobby as 'Anglophobia'. What a noxious little idiot he was. Hopefully, his spirit wanders the glens still, seeking desperately to borrow thruppence.

William McIllvanney

There is one Scottish joke or reference we hear from non-Scots frequently, more frequently perhaps than its nearest competitor, the joke in which the teller adopts a comedy accent to point out that it's a 'braw bricht moonlicht nicht the nicht' (translation: tonight the moon is shining brightly). That joke was from the Morecambe and Wise era. Its successor is more recent. It involves the teller adopting a comedy accent to declare that 'There's been a murrr-derr!' We know what the joke is alluding to; to the TV detective drama *Taggart*, set in Glasgow, in which dead bodies pile up like cattle. The quip is rueful acknowledgement of the perception that life in Glasgow is red in tooth and claw, attenuated often by the feral instincts of the locals.

However, the comment did not feature in an episode of *Taggart*. It was drawn from somewhere else entirely and attributed to the television drama by a kind of sympathetic osmosis. It comes, in fact, from page twenty-seven of *Laidlaw*, a novel written in 1977: '"There's been a murder," he said. Ena paused over the vegetables she was chopping for Monday's soup.' Though predating the television series by several years, the novel was as close to *Taggart* as made no difference. Each helped coin the style that has bedevilled the nation ever since, and which in recent years has come to be known as tartan noir. Like bindweed, tartan noir has run rampant.

The bulk of Scottish novels now are sub-Chandler things in which maverick detectives and forensic pathologists put tags on toes while musing upon the state of the nation.

And the blame can be traced back, like a revolver with an intact serial number, to William McIllvanney, author of *Laidlaw* and of any number of novels in which hard-drinking loners find themselves at odds with their superiors. This is possibly unfair on McIllvanney. Formerly he was a proper literary novelist and poet. He produced only a trilogy of Laidlaw books then hung up his raincoat and returned to proper writing. But *Laidlaw* was seminal and its children were profuse: from Denise Mina to Christopher Brookmyre, from Val McDermid to Ian Rankin. The name of Scotland's game became genre fiction, in which rookie police officers threw up on seeing their first dismembered body; in which ex-wives despaired at the predilection of their former partners for emotional pain; in which a thousand glasses of Scotch were thrown back while a thousand internal monologues rambled on. Thanks to McIllvanney's example an entire generation of writers was lost to this stuff. There was, indeed, a murder, and McIllvanney wielded the claw-hammer.

Charles Rennie Mackintosh

Were you visit to Glasgow, board one of the city's dinky subway trains and alight at Hillhead station in the west end, a pleasant surprise would await. Underground stations on the whole tend to be drab, utilitarian spaces, but not this one. Its entrance hall is a riot of line and colour. Along the length of one wall is a dramatic mural depicting a God's-eye view of the surrounding locale, beneath a roiling sky of the darkest blue. Local characters have been included, alongside a menagerie of mythical beasts. Created by the artist and novelist Alasdair Gray, the mural is an altogether daring and commendable creation, a credit to the city and to the country.

Let us rewind two years, however, to a meeting of the city council. On the agenda: a proposal to modernise the city's fifteen subway stations, which having lain untouched since 1980 are by now markedly tatty. It is decided that this is a splendid idea. Thoughts turn to the design style the stations might adopt. Heads are scratched. Pen tops are chewed. An air of deep concentration descends. All is silent, until the voice of a lone councillor pipes up: 'We'll just do it Mackintosh, yes?'

The name Charles Rennie Mackintosh strikes fear into most Scottish hearts, even if the man himself was an unlikely villain, an architect and designer, 1868 to 1928. He merits opprobrium because, thanks to the laziness and caution of others, his style became endemic, ubiquitous, omnipresent, to a point where the sole group not heartily sickened by him were nice old pensioners. Mackintosh was the ultimate victim of his own success, though Glasgow city councillors played their role. Few in Glasgow had given much thought to Mackintosh, to his pleasingly angular buildings or his Art Nouveau furniture, since the 1920s. He was merely another hirsute Victorian on the tapestry of Glasgow antiquity.

This changed in 1990 when the city became the European Capital of Culture and set about scouring the civic attic for local bric-a-brac. Among the finds was Mackintosh: forgotten at home but rated by significant figures like Frank Lloyd Wright, as an artisan whose work was delicate and decorative. Glasgow rehabilitated him with gusto. Mackintosh had designed his own typeface and it was dusted off to become the year's official visual language, with its elongated lines and triple-bars on the letters A and H. It was reminiscent of the Jazz Age and Art Deco, but had something *mitteleuropean* to it also, something redolent of men named Bela sketching in grand-cafés. The style was perfect for Glasgow's year in the European spotlight, particularly given the city's reputation for violence and squalor. Mackintosh ticked every box: his style was inherently Glaswegian; it was sophisticated yet familiar, posh but pleasing. Quickly, it was everywhere, from T-shirts to flower beds. You visited a restaurant: the posters in the widow were written with Mackintosh, the menus used Mackintosh and the signs on the toilet doors. Mackintosh furniture was revived too. In cafés and restaurants copies began appearing of his high-backed chairs and lozenge-shaped tables. Rose motifs were inlaid into panes of glass; twisty wrought iron appeared on every public bannister. Overnight, living in Glasgow came to feel like living in a Gustav Klimt postcard.

Before long, the style was exported around Scotland. It started doing turns for coffee shops in Inverness, jewellers in Dundee, picture-framers in Perth. Each time you stepped into the cashmered, sucky-sweet realm of the over-sixties you confronted a bit of Mackintosh. He became progenitor of Scotland's design *lingua franca*. For the best part of two decades Mackintosh was nigh-on unavoidable, a blight, a joke; visual proof of Scotland's complacency, its fondness for the familiar. Modern Scotland had found the guy to dot its i's and cross its t's and, by God, it was sticking with him.

A century earlier, Mackintosh would have been flattered, but then he would have been flattered by anything short of arrest. His story was archetypically Scottish, a maudlin narrative of illness, poverty and thwarted progress; a sob story. Only a handful of his designs were built in his lifetime. The remainder stayed on the drawing board, like architectural IOUs. In recent years a number of these designs have been built, even if the families meant to live in them went nearly a century back to meet, as Mackintosh did, the greatest Architect of all. You do have to feel sorry for the fellow; in life he floundered, then enjoyed the briefest of vogues, then became so hackneyed that the tide turned again.

Things were different in 1895 when Mackintosh while still a humble draughtsman at Honeyman & Keppie was lauded for designing the Glasgow *Herald* building, a foretaste of his solid yet sensual style. Mackintosh was at work as two schools were developing independently, Modernism and Japonism, tendencies he converged in designs that were artistic but accessible, and dismissive of architecture's classical tradition. He designed several further major buildings in or near Glasgow but his career was short, ending around 1916, when shortage of work drove him to London and a new life as a watercolourist. From there he and his wife Margaret went to Port-Vendres, a town in southern France. Cancer drove him back to London where he died aged sixty.

By rights, of course, Mackintosh himself can't be held responsible for his eventual dismaying ubiquity. He was long dead. But his name has taken on an incantatory power, wholly out of proportion to the stature he earned by his day job; so much so the name was adapted colloquially to suggest the horrors of his overuse. Copies of his work became known as Mockintosh. In Glasgow these days you will hear the term Mockintosh more commonly than you will the dread name of Mackintosh. The designer has become the definition of a busted flush, a blunted pencil. He is to Scotland what Donald McGill is to the English seaside: groaningly predictable and now horribly vulgar.

But his legacy lingers still, expressed in the councillors who hoped to give Rennie Mackintosh one more go on the city's subway trains, before their folly was explained by younger, more clued-in colleagues. If nothing else, the incident was salutary. It reminded us to be ever-watchful, and certain that wherever two or three undiscriminitating Scottish pensioners are gathered the work of Charles Rennie Mackintosh will be close by, with yet further designs on our patience.

Colin Montgomerie

Golf. Naturally we know what the word means – but we know also what it connotes. Golf isn't merely a sport; it is a cult, a lifestyle, a philosophy. But, principally, it's a curse. Golf caddies round the fairway of existence, its huge Slazenger bag crammed with scorn and prejudice, for only golfers take golf in any way seriously. Mark Twain set the small, pitted ball rolling when he is said to have described golf as 'a good walk spoiled'. The author and broadcaster Alistair Cooke chimed in with this: 'In golf, humiliations are the essence of the game.' Golf is where the male libido goes when it dies. Think about men; their get-up-and-go, the ingenuity and vigour they bring to their professional life, all that curiosity and purpose. Then they wake up and realise the fan belt has snapped, that the motor is idling; that hurly-burly matters less than once it did. Suddenly, that sweater in the window of BHS, the one with purple diamonds edged in orange, becomes rather appealing. Like a doctor watching in a microscope the division of malignant cells, we are witnessing a strange and terrible genesis; the birth of a golfer.

Golfers, however, are oblivious to the mocking laughter. They just don't get what we don't get about golf. As well they might. Golf is the only sport whose practitioners we pity. We look at tennis players, by contrast, and we admire the speed and strength,

the agility and the cunning. We look at footballers and envy the high-rolling golden-child lifestyles. With rugby players we respond to the physical fortitude, as we do with boxers. We look at golfers, though, and we bite our bottom lips hard, as our mirth-moistened eyes transmit the urgent necessity of having the subject changed.

Golfers are the clowns, the harlequins of the sporting realm. Which is not to imply they are flamboyant or arresting. Rather, the lesser-spotted golfer is characterised by his banality, by his clubbable, comfort-fit middle-management mildness; by his sandals-with-socks, dad-dancing, *Daily Mail*-crossword awfulness. He has the air of a man with seed catalogues in the glove box of his Audi and gloves in the pockets of his lime-green jerkin. Added to which, golf is bi-polar, schizophrenic. Golf is the sporting equivalent of a hair-weave or sunglasses on the over-forties, it exists in defiance of the onset of male saplessness. Yet the sport is a celebration of the same saplessness, a pretext for fleeing into a safe, placid bloke-womb of stats, averages, equipment and accoutrements. A properly sensible person wouldn't even *think* of becoming a golfer, not for all the tee in China.

Scotland, though, sadly, invented golf and, even sadder still, she felt it necessary to embody and personify golf, in the less-than-svelte shape of Colin Montgomerie, a shape that puts the mockers on any belief in the efficiency of intelligent design. You merely look at Montgomerie, with his slacks and club tie, his equine teeth and astroturf hair, and develop the urge to ensure your tax return is in order. Untypically for a Scottish sportsman it isn't a woeful sporting record that renders Montgomerie so resistible. As a player he was really quite effective, with an impressive Ryder Cup record: he won thirty-one European tour events, more than any British player, and won the PGA Championship at Wentworth three years consecutively. At one point he was ranked second finest player on earth. During 2013 he was inducted into the World Golf Hall of Fame.

Though born in Scotland, in Dunning, Perthshire, Montgomerie was raised in Yorkshire, where his father was managing director of the company that made Fox's Biscuits. Altogether, it must have been a horrid double-whammy: to learn you're from Yorkshire just as you develop an interest in golf. It never rains but it pars. But who knows? Maybe these are the factors necessary to make a character as chippy (pardon the golf pun), driven (likewise), bumptious, arrogant and as faintly comic as Colin Montgomerie.

To gain a sense of this, we return to 2004 and a press conference for some tournament or other. Montgomerie had only recently, and publicly, split from his first wife Eimear, for reasons to which we shall return. Montgomerie had found himself, as celebrities say, *in a bad place*. Perfectly understandable, one supposes. Nothing is as sad as a lonely golfer. The protracted and ambulatory nature of the sport means competitors are obliged to spend long hours in one another's company, discussing the glories of central locking and Theresa May. Their competitors are pre-occupied equally by automotive technology and Tory dominatrixes, so it all works out rather well, which explains why they find golf so compelling.

And then you are exposed to the comfort of strangers, which can test anyone's emotional fortitude. At the press conference Montgomerie was told by a young female reporter, Jane Lewis of BBC Scotland, that he was looking very relaxed. Rather than attributing his ease to an unusually comfy sweater or the smooth running of his new Renault Mégane, Montgomerie, in full view of television cameras, chose to make a clumsy pass: 'Thank you very much,' he replied wolfishly. 'Can I give you my address?'

An entire nation felt a ghost walk over its grave. Momentarily, Lewis considered the prospect of a lifetime's free access to the jacuzzi at the Wentworth Spa Centre but pulled back just in time and declined to respond. Let us ponder for a moment the thought process that allowed this exchange. Montgomerie has heard that he is looking 'relaxed'. A non-golfer might interpret this as meaning they appeared rested or comfortable. Montgomerie, however, took it as meaning that he was hunky, sexy, irresistible, or all three simultaneously.

The incident wasn't wholly out of left field. Montgomerie has pursued the kind of love life capable of shaming a bonobo chimp. His mashie niblick was forever seeking new lockers in which to rest. Indeed, some of Montgomerie's liaisons have taken place at times when the laws of the land – specifically the Marriage Act of 1949 – placed no restriction upon his behaviour. But randiness is seldom a gracious or appealing quality, and with Montgomerie it merely compounds the prevailing impression, that of an arrogant, self-regarding, supercharged bank manager whose soul wears Hush Puppies.

Let us crack out the flow chart and attempt to follow recent years in its life. In 1990, aged twenty-six, Montgomerie married Eimear, with whom he had three children and stayed with until 2006. Two years earlier the marriage had begun to break down and, after a fling with Inès Sastre, someone the papers dubbed 'golfer and supermodel', he commenced an affair with one Joanne Baldwin, a woman he'd met on the school run. That relationship floundered, though, with news of Montgomerie's relationship with television presenter Alison Walker. In 2008, he married millionaire widow Gaynor Knowles at Loch Lomond. Yet, as ever, the bunker beckoned and months after the wedding Montgomerie was revealed to be trying for a birdie with Ms Baldwin once more. 'I have put my marriage under considerable strain,' was his masterfully blank *mea culpa*. None of this was admirable, lovable or even raffish. It was merely, as with everything connected with Montgomerie, dispiriting and so awfully, awfully suburban.

Andy Murray

You want to know what differentiates the Scots from the English? Church bells. That's what truly separates the tribes. Those clanging calls to pew-bound prayer. The difference between church bells in Scotland and church bells in England is the difference between hell and heaven, between the Old Testament Jehovah and meek, gentle Jesus.

Imagine it is a Sunday morning in England, anywhere from, say, Warwickshire down to Land's End. The chances are you've been woken by the weekly fusillade; that, as John Betjeman put it, you have been summoned to consciousness by bells. Largely, this is a pleasant experience, regardless of your position on religion. English churches still practice change-ringing, that appealing swirl of chimes and peals we associate with Whitsun weddings and happy news about the old King. To hear change-ringing does something agreeable to the soul. We link the sound with encouraging announcements and new beginnings. Also, we can't help visualising how the noise is being made to issue forth, all those good people of the parish bungeeing up and down on bell ropes in the manner familiar from a thousand Sunday evening sit-coms. For the broadsheet-reading middle-classes of middle England this is how the week ends: in a welter of pleasing noise, sacred but ever-so nice. Whereas in Scotland all we get is the

unadorned, fearful *dong* of the Presbytery bell, like a policeman at the door with bad news.

It is not difficult to identify the reason for this: the Scottish reformation. Probably there were fears that making such melodious cheer issue from the house of God might lead to sexual intercourse or, even worse, to dancing. In 1560, the ringing of bells in churches was discontinued in Scotland, other than for the most functional purposes of indicating the commencement of a service. The Presbyterian church was established in 1690, its style markedly more austere than the Anglicans in the south. The Presbyterians were admirable in many ways, particularly for their distaste for the lurid mysteries of Rome, but this particular edict was something of an own goal. It denied Scotland one of the civilising pleasantries of English life, one of the flakes of fairy dust that makes urban life in England so much nicer than it is in Scotland. The stricture applies still. There are a handful of places in Scotland where change-ringing *can* be heard but, largely, Scotland on a Sunday morning sounds much as it did during the reign of Bloody Mary. And this has had an effect on the Scottish soul. It renders it drier, quieter, duller, less likely to dance upon the village green in jester's cap waving a bladder on a stick. It has swathed in velvet the clapper of national character.

And if one person exemplifies this muted and muffled strain in the Scottish psyche Andy Murray is that person. No matter the heights of professional success or remunerative splendour to which Murray climbs he continues to give the impression that moments earlier he barked his shin on a coffee table. Few in the public arena refuse so doggedly to pin a grin above their chin. Watching Murray interviewed *après*-match is like witnessing a suicidal undertaker describe the shortcomings of his cross-court backhand. You itch to scream at him: 'Cheer up, you Caledonian muppet!' before appreciating the inherent inconsistencies of such an attitude.

Murray, famously, grew up in Dunblane, and this explains a lot. The little town, roughly equidistant between Glasgow and Edinburgh, is as douce and decent as any hamlet could be. The civic flag was knitted from a cashmere-viscose blend and shows a pair of crossed Audis on a backing of heraldic azure. The village isn't built for emotional exuberance. None of this endears Murray to the English, who find him as morose and resistible as someone sleeping in a Tube station doorway. This is bad for Scots, of course, but it is worse for the English. The latter, as we know, are starved of sporting success, to a degree that's really quite excruciating to witness, so total is the fug of self-delusion that descends over sporting occasions in which the English have an interest. Meanwhile, in the previous few years, it had become obvious that Murray had all the makings of a Wimbledon champion. The English revere Wimbledon as druids revere the summer solstice. It was only to be expected Murray would be grasped to the national bosom. But things haven't worked out like this. The English look upon Murray as recovering alcoholics look upon litre bottles of single malt: tempting, compelling but, all things considered, best kept at arm's length even after he became, in 2013, the first Briton in 77 years to win the Wimbledon title. Such an impulse is implied in the formulation that irks Scots most, as used, we claim, in so much media coverage of Murray's career: when he succeeds he is described as *British* tennis player Andy Murray; and when he has failed as a *Scottish* tennis player.

Whatever the truth, the ambivalence the English feel for Murray clearly has roots in the new political settlement arrived at in 1997, mixed with vestiges of the derision southern England has always reserved for the Jocks. As a conspicuous Scot, one with the temerity to prosper in a sport the English hold to be theirs, Murray became a lightning rod for how England had been made to feel by the rewriting of the affiliation: bruised, scandalised, defiant. The relationship has never been an easy one; to this day BBC commentators at Wimbledon still refer pointedly to Henman Hill in preference to its more recent designation, Murray Mount. Matters took a marked turn for the worse in 2010 when Murray was asked during a television interview who he planned to support in the forthcoming World Cup campaign (for which his home country had not qualified) and replied 'Anyone but England'. The remark provoked divergent responses. In Scotland Murray all but received a ticker-tape parade. In England, he was vilified. The reaction continues to condition English responses to Murray, even after his victory in the US Open and his gold in the London Olympics. The levity of the comment has been forgiven but never forgotten. Suspicion remains that Murray at heart is a *Daily Mail* cartoon of a Scot, warming his hands round the flame of a candle while hatching plans to annex Cumbria.

He probably isn't. Probably Murray is a typical modern Scot: proud of his roots, unfussed about our friends in the south, quietly pleased to be living through a period when the historico-political account is being checked and balanced. If anything, his anyone-but-England remark was pro-English. When it comes to their national team, the English have a Cycloptic blind spot. The culture surrounding the English national team is definitively noxious: all that rapey, spit-roasting, coon-baiting camaraderie; all the selective quotation of statistics English commentators use to prove that England will this year definitely win the thing they're competing for; all the beefy, bullish bemusement of fans when they don't. They each sound frothingly, moon-huggingly, preorgasmically deranged. Culturally, this isn't England; it's Essex. England is the most gorgeous, glorious place in the history of the planet. Sadly, though, it seems to have outsourced its elite football to eleven millionaire nightclub bouncers with Tourette's. One imagines it was this version of England Murray was slighting. And the attack was perfectly justified. Conversely, you won't find any argument here as regards Murray's own deficiencies, most particularly his surliness and downheartedness, tendencies that reinforce and perpetuate a very old and resented Scottish stereotype, that of the chippy malcontent, the human no-fly zone, the cautious, funereal prig. So ask not for whom the bell tolls; it tolls for Andy.

Nick Nairn

When the sad day arrives and Nick Nairn takes that long walk into the white light of eternal rest, his grave will be topped with a stone on which two words will be carved: Celebrity Chef. It is what Nairn is, was and ever will be. As such, though, he was always a tad untypical, a bit off-menu. He never really had an angle, a hook. He wasn't unblinking and cerebral like Heston Blumenthal or free-range posh like Hugh Fearnley- Whittingstall. His cleavage never rivalled that of Nigella Lawson. Nairn was neither kooky nor singular. He was a caterer whose profile came to the boil, then subsided. He was human tofu, nutritious but flavourless; merely an agreeable bloke from Stirlingshire who hoped to finish his shift, you felt, in time to get to a television and watch the Six Nations.

When he was among the first wave of television chefs, back when the popular cookery racket was in its salad days, this amiability served Nairn well. Hitherto, cookery on television had been a strange and esoteric realm, ruled by 70-per-cent-proof fruitcakes like Fanny Cradock or camp aesthetes such as Graham Kerr, the so-called Galloping Gourmet. Over the genre hung the floury, lumpy, indigestible pall of the home economics class. Television cookery skulked in the afternoon schedules, loved no more than contemporaneous shows concerning fretwork or painting in watercolours. Then along came Nick and colleagues to tell us that making a proper prawn cocktail was no trickier than taxing the Land Rover or sourcing a really chunky pair of corduroys.

All this was some time ago, though. It is twenty-five years since Nairn became the youngest Scottish chef to win a Michelin star and twenty since he became a regular on *Ready Steady Cook*, the daytime BBC cookery challenge. In terms of serious reputation, Nairn is a bit wilted now. These days, his vague, thumbs-up to local and seasonal produce philosophy seems merely a bowlful of the bleeding obvious. However, do not assume that Nairn is overly bothered. He isn't. He has moved on. He's a businessman now, up to his oxters in consultancy and retail diffusion, trade shows and cookery schools. Give him a whisk, you suspect, and he'll try phoning his agent with it.

Yet even when his reputation was at boiling point, Nairn was a less than inspiring figure. This seemed counterintuitive, given that the very point of a television cookery guru is to be inspirational, to galvanise the viewer to grasp the rudiments. The best television chefs have strategies for doing so. Jamie Oliver is voluble and enthusiastic, like someone hoping they'll make you sign a Direct Debit for Mencap. Rick Stein is Ahab's stunt double, with a soul soaked in brine. Nigella Lawson is sensual and licks the ingredients from her fingers, except when making black pudding. In contrast, Nairn spent his days in rain-lashed field of curly kale, declaiming 'My, that's a fine specimen!' There was no real passion or individuality or quirkiness to Nairn, as there was to, say, Clarissa Dickson Wright or the Hairy Bikers; none of Keith Floyd's pop-eyed mischief nor Delia Smith's prim propriety; none of whatever Antony Worrall-Thompson had, whatever that was. He was a housewives' favourite, with all the narcoleptic agreeability the term implies.

For Nairn was cooking up a different plan. He wanted out of the trenches and into the corridors of power. He was to pursue a crucial, though self-appointed, role in what would effectively become Scotland's finger-wagging ministry of dietary responsibility, constituted along with the minority Nationalist administration in 2007. As soon as Nairn had made his name he became the mouthpiece through which this new culinary orthodoxy was expressed. Scotland was the sick man of Europe and Nairn was to be his doctor, or at least the bloke in charge of the hospital kitchen. From him came a fusillade of crawly endorsements in support of whatever happened that week to be getting the Scottish government's bib in a twist: healthy diets, fish farms, unhealthy diets, food sustainability, fast food, fishing quotas, school dinners – you name it and Nairn was happy to be photographed beside a loch, appearing thoughtful about it.

Rather quickly this became nauseating. As did the very sight of the fellow; photographed, invariably, in his chef's whites, grin so wide he resembled the joker on finding £20 in an old pair of trousers, his neat and tidy office-boy looks setting off nicely his tartan trews. The grin was scarcely surprising; like a well-made soufflé the Nairn brand was rising nicely. Soon he was establishing cook schools and newspaper sinecures, a television series, a range of books. His cook schools offered ranges of Nick Nairn merchandise: a branded chopping board scraper at £9.99, anyone? He became a presenter on the BBC farming series *Landward*. He cooked an eightieth-birthday dinner for Queen Elizabeth II. He received an honorary doctorate from Stirling University. Whenever pot clanked against pan up popped Nairn like a genie from a bottle, par-boiling with bright ideas.

But still the question simmered – what, actually, was the point of Nick Nairn? What was his contribution to the culinary arts;

what type of thumbprint was he leaving on the puff pastry of posterity? What legacy was he leaving, beyond a number of well-provisioned trust funds? What was his signature flourish, his great stylistic innovation? Any television chef worth their sea-salt tends to have one. Blumenthal had molecular gastronomy; Ramsay adapted French classicism for British palates, and swore; Lawson did her super-charged Delia Smith thing. They sang for our suppers, they brought something to the table. But Nairn? Not so much. It dawned gradually that Nairn was a cook rather than a chef; a skilled technician but no visionary, with no argument to make, no artistry in his approach to food. Nairn seldom met a beef joint he didn't like, nor fail to prepare in the most traditional fashion possible.

All this, of course, had a trickle-down effect. Elsewhere in Britain, the early years of the 21st century saw some kind of culinary rebirth, catalysed in part by the television chefs, by the Sunday supplements and, responding to demand, by the supermarkets. The phenomenon was centred on London but it came to radiate outwards. Until, that is, it reached the border whereupon Nairn's baleful influence reasserted itself. In 2010 he made his biggest statement of intent yet when he launched a restaurant named the Kailyard within the Dunblane Hydro hotel.

Its menu was an almost parodic litany of the over-familiar and the done-to-death: ham hock, chicken liver parfait, pork belly, fish pie, steak, gnocchi for the vegetarians. Each was astonishingly unpleasant; grim, production-line swill churned out with the utmost in parsimonious cynicism. What was described as slow-roasted pork belly, Stornoway black pudding, apple and crispy bacon salad came as a cube of fearsomely dry, chewy matter overwhelmed by a sauce resembling melted Curly Wurly. The fish pie was unremarkable ready-meal-style fare, but it contained

'seasonal market fish', a claim that provokes most to ask how fish
can be seasonal, given they live in the sea, which, by definition, is
season-free. But the description sounded right and that was the
main thing. 'Nick's own recipe char-grilled cheese burger' was a
rubbery beer mat in a bleached industrial bun with processed
cheese. What was worse, though, was looking upon the diners, who
were clearly accustomed to more modest surroundings, blithe in
the assumption that their proximity to a celebrity chef meant they
were living the high life. Like the food, the thought was just too
melancholy to bear. Making one realise that Nairn has been pulling
the same trick on the whole of Scotland for many years now.

Gordon Ramsay

In 1997, the BBC began screening a situation comedy entitled *I'm Alan Partridge*. Its titular character was a regional radio presenter who'd lucked a stint as a television chat show host, only to flounder on the rocks of woeful incompetence. Having been sacked, Partridge meets with his former boss to pitch new programme ideas. These are not merely poor but poor in ways that expose his utter desperation: *Swallow*, for example, an anti-vandalism detective series set in Norwich; or *Alan Attack*, hard-hitting investigative journalism 'with a more slapstick approach'. The boss is unimpressed. Partridge panics. *Arm-Wrestling with Chas and Dave*? *Inner-City Sumo*? Not a flicker of interest. Improvising wildly, Partridge pulls a suggestion from the depths of his fevered imagination: *Cooking In Prison*. Quite properly, the boss looks horrified.

However, life was to imitate art. The idea of a television show titled *Cooking In Prison* was thought so crass it assumed a culty life of its own, became a meme. It was referenced in conversations and newspaper articles. It became a synonym for the bottom-dredging opportunism of contemporary television formats. Informally, to those in the know, *Cooking In Prison* came to be considered among the worst format ideas ever conceived. Fast-forward to June 2012 and the release, or escape perhaps, of a new series on Channel Four, *Gordon Behind Bars*. In this quite

unconnected series, Gordon Ramsay, the combative, expletive-hurling chef, taught the rudiments of cookery to inmates at Brixton prison. In the modern television fashion a measure of jeopardy was deemed necessary, and introduced by means of a spurious deadline; Ramsay and his jailbirds had just six months to set up their own food business. A tall order, even if they were excused the obligation of offering a home delivery service. The viewer couldn't help thinking the artificial tension a touch superfluous. A foul-mouthed millionaire was to share confined space with convicts and a range of sharp implements; who could guess what manner of retribution might await the appalling Ramsay? One opted to let nature take its course and switched over to BBC4.

Those viewers who remained, though, were dining out for weeks afterwards on the faint aftertaste of *schadenfreude*. Surely this was a turning point, the moment at which the resistible Ramsay finally ran out of road? It couldn't have come sooner. Since 1998, Ramsay had been serving up on television a gamey menu; of derision, bullying, aggression and language heard more commonly from those who've dipped an earlobe in the deep-fat fryer. Ramsay became the defining TV celebrity chef, in the way Patrick Moore became the defining TV astronomer or Tony Blackburn the defining TV disc jockey. In sketch-show satires and newspaper cartoons Ramsay was invariably the model used as TV chef, as three decades earlier Fanny Cradock was. He became an archetype, immediately identifiable and therefore, happily, imme-diately avoidable; Ramsay, with his hair of tousled blonde, lending him resemblance to a roadie for rock group The Police circa 1979; his scarred chin like a diagram of a tram interchange; his expression one of constant, simmering annoyance.

There was a further difficulty: Ramsay's competence as a chef was something most were obliged to take on trust. He cooks for an expense-account crowd only. With Ramsay there are no thirty-minute-meals, no explorations of hearty peasant cuisines, as you get with Jamie or Nigella. Ramsay could no more catch and gut a mackerel than he could levitate. Instead, he is imperial, top-level, blue ribbon. For Ramsay, *haute cuisine* is never *haute* enough. His menus are forbidding, high-walled Bastilles of *velouté*, *ventrèche* and *vacherin*. His set lunches read like the cast list of *Les Misérables*. This is perfectly explicable, in its way; Ramsay is a chef rather than a cook. But, thus, his oddity becomes even greater. Which is the real Ramsay – the purist, the restless, temperamental virtuoso gaining the higher reaches of his art? Or the one-trick television pony, bawling out his underlings? The maestro or the comedy thug? The genius or the twat?

We need only look at what Ramsay has become. There was a time he was respectable professionally, stood shoulder to shoulder with the big beasts of France. Those days are long gone. His restaurants survive, of course, but they're infra-dig now, fixtures on the tourist trail, like Madame Tussauds or *The Mousetrap*, administrated by a vast holding company and as personally acquainted with their progenitor as a burger bar is with Ronald McDonald. Ramsay belongs now more properly to the tabloid world, a realm of red carpets and celebrity endorsement. He fills the trough at which the great unhosed tuck in and pig out. Ramsay exists to front increasingly threadbare television formats: Gordon shouts at dismal restaurateurs (*Ramsay's Kitchen Nightmares*); Gordon shouts at foreign restaurateurs (*Gordon's Great Escape*); Gordon shouts at guests in a hotel (*Hotel GB*). Ramsay now is merely a brand, a culinary kite mark, signifying that at any moment the unwary and the inept will be upbraided by a trained professional of infinitely greater competence. Ramsay's act has become like a psychotic edition of *The Generation Game*, with amateurs sneered at for their tentative way of braising a shallot. Yet he is reminiscent also of a 1970s actor, a hellraiser like Richard Burton or Richard Harris, a histrionic monster, a conspicuous maniac, clinging to well-remunerated shlock amid the ruins of a once-respectable career.

He who lives by the newspaper profile and the first-night invite dies by them. Such has come to pass for Ramsay. A persona that at first seemed bracingly forthright became in time unedifying and pathological. Ramsay's personal and professional worlds began to crumble away. His claim to have played three matches for the first team of Rangers Football Club was revealed to contain all the truth of *Roy of the Rovers*. In 2004 he closed Amaryllis, his only restaurant in his birth city of Glasgow, claiming, rather snootily, that the city was not yet ready for fine dining. In 2008, a Sunday tabloid revealed the married Ramsay had been conducting three secret affairs. Shortly after, his father-in-law Chris Hutcheon left his position as CEO of Gordon Ramsey Holdings amid accusations of infidelity and embezzlement. Ramsay, Hutcheon claimed, was a 'friendless egotist'.

Cooking on television used to be such a placid, ennobling thing. The ladies in *Farmhouse Kitchen* were forever up to their floury elbows in flans. Johnny would show us how to make doughnuts like Fanny's. What Delia Smith didn't know about separating egg whites wasn't worth knowing. The genre was both diverting and practical. Then, suddenly, the timer pinged and it was time for Ramsay to come out of the oven.

Before we knew it, police sirens were howling, bodies were being slammed against fridge doors and ingenious uses were being suggested for the bacon scissors. We were in a brave new world; of screaming matches, jump-cuts, head-to-head confrontations, secret filming, tearful breakdowns. The full armoury of the modern televisual method was deployed, with all its anxiety and red-blooded hyperkineticism. Ramsay's colleagues and assistants were belittled. Diners were stared out. A death-or-glory mindset was inculcated, one that advocated an ultra-serious, sinew-stretching attitude to absolutely everything. Like a FCUK t-shirt, Ramsay coarsened, he deepened the vulgarity of everyday life.

We'd suggest prison. But he beat us to it.

Lord Reith

'That Wuthering Height' was the nickname Sir Winston Churchill gave John Charles Walsham Reith, 1st Baron Reith, referencing the Emily Brontë novel in which some northerners learn just how harsh life can be. The description was apposite. At six foot six Reith was unusually tall, while *wuthering* was a Yorkshire term for a chilling wind. Reith always stood apart, both by dint of his physical scale and by the effects he exerted. This was in the 1930s. Back then, Reith was the founder and first Director-General of the British Broadcasting Corporation. He had no shortage of detractors. He has more today.

Posterity has not been kind to Lord Reith. He looms from the past, in suit of Bible-black, unblinking, unsmiling, like Great Britain's headmaster, the very embodiment of grey eminence, as cuddly as a thistle, bent and blasted now by gales of public derision. In our mind's ear we can hear his flinty, grumpy vowels, heavy with Free Church rectitude. We picture him declaiming and forbidding and preventing. Reith trademarked the modern idea of the Scot, as God-fearing prude and spiritual miser. Hitherto, when people thought of the Scots, they pictured kilts and combative Highlanders, they saw colourful and kinetic characters. Reith changed all that. He made Scottishness something altogether drearier. After Reith, a new caricature gained currency: the

Scotsman as joyless invigilator, as cultural chaperone, cold, cautious and cheerless, allergic to all levity and ostentation. Similar figures had long appeared in Scottish literature: the minister in 'Holy Willie's Prayer' by Robert Burns, for example, who attempts to have a parishioner charged for travelling on the Sabbath, or in James Hogg's *The Private Memoirs and Confessions of a Justified Sinner*. Reith took the type overground, added it to the lexicon, he publicised and popularised it. His name, like that of Churchill, ironically enough, has become an adjective; we speak of Reithian values and know the term suggests a certain type of high-minded austerity. Lord Reith became, in effect, the first, and perhaps the only, celebrity Presbyterian.

Not, however, that Lord Reith was to have much involvement in, say, *Bruce Forsyth's Generation Game* or *The Flower Pot Men*. Reith loathed and deplored television, termed it an 'abomination' and, anyway, he departed the Corporation in 1938, in the earliest days of its television service. What we think of as Reithian values never applied to the medium with which we connect them, television. Rather, the Reithian strictures related to radio. On Sundays BBC stations did not commence broadcasting until 12.30 p.m. in order that listeners have time to attend church; even at that, programmes following were restricted to religious services and classical music. It is difficult to conceive of a man less fitted to this new medium, as Reith himself was not the last to admit, recalling in his autobiography early days 'confronted with problems of which I had no experience: copyright and performing rights; Marconi patents; associations of concert artists, authors, playwrights, composers, music publishers, theatre managers, wireless manufacturers.' Such was to be expected perhaps given that, previously, there had been nowhere to learn such ropes. However, Reith had negotiated successful careers in the army, serving in the

First World War, in armament supply and in engineering. This background, part mechanical, part administrative, rendered him suitable for a post advertised in 1922 for General Manager of the British Broadcasting Company, proposed by an alliance of radio manufacturers. His only preparation for his job interview was prayer: 'They didn't ask me many questions and some they did I didn't know the meaning of,' Reith would recall. 'The fact is I hadn't the remotest idea as to what broadcasting was. I hadn't troubled to find out. If I had tried I should probably have found difficulty in discovering anyone who knew.'

Reith secured the post but his background wouldn't allow him to facilitate without resentment anything so frivolous as mere entertainment. He had been raised in Glasgow as a son of the manse, his father a minister in the United Free Church of Scotland. It may be you aren't up to speed with the many-headed Hydra that is Scottish Presbyterianism. Suffice to say that while the United Free Church falls some way short of the grim hardline rigour of the original Free Church it won't be organising any wet T-shirt contests in the near future. The upbringing left Reith militantly pious (publicly at least) and morally exacting. Among BBC staff extra-marital affairs resulted in dismissal, as did divorce. He ruled the Corporation with a whim of iron; for example prohibiting use of the term famous as an adjective, on the grounds that if the word was being used accurately it was by definition unnecessary and if it was being used hyperbolically it was misleading.

It is difficult to assess Reith's legacy fully, given that his function was to edit and prevent, not to act and innovate. It is the bureaucrat's curse: influence without acknowledgement. We can no longer see what Reith did. We hear only the faintest echo of his gloomy, stentorian voice. He hides in plain sight. He is known to us in caricature only, as the first comic Scot to follow Sir Harry Lauder, and the template of so many gloomy willies to come. In many ways he was akin to those men who once walked ahead of automobiles waving warning flags. He was useful in the early days of the Corporation, then easy to do without. So was Reith famous? Or just notorious?

The latter, principally; nothing pleasant ever attached itself to Lord Reith. He was the original cloud on a sunny day, the man who ran the fledgling BBC as though it was a Sunday school on Stornoway. It was a measure of Reith's regard for his own assurance, and of his estrangement from the public he served, that he could express support for Hitler, having seen in him a kindred respect of brusque purpose: 'I am pretty certain,' Reith wrote in 1933, 'that the Nazis will clean things up and put Germany on the way to being a real power in Europe again. They are being ruthless and most determined.'

Posthumously, Reith completed the bounder checklist in 2007 when his daughter Marista Leishman disclosed he had been an appalling father: distant, spiteful and wrathful. Lustful too, despite his strenuously maintained facade of Calvinist mortification. Throughout his life Reith pursued an ambiguous alliance with boyhood friend Charlie Bowser, with whom he and a girl named Muriel established a triangular relationship: 'In some crazy way,' Marista told reporters, 'he thought if he was married to her, it would regularise what he had with Charlie.' Later Reith would settle into more conventional patterns of infidelity, with BBC secretaries and the like. He was keeping his end up, so to speak, even at the age of seventy. He died aged eighty-one, back in Scotland. His ashes were interred in the grounds of a church near Inverness, thus at least lending his life a unity of theme, a pleasing circularity. It was typical of this resistible, draconian extremist that he declined to do any such pleasing while still alive.

J.K. Rowling

At first glance, at fifth glance even, author J.K. Rowling seems a blameless soul. Lovely Joanne, with her Rapunzel hair of strawberry-blonde and her primary-teacher bearing, her fabric-softened soul. At any moment, you feel, she'll request you cover your text-books in wallpaper then draw a map of the solar system. What objection could be raised against Joanne? The mission is not easy, like setting out to mow down a lollipop lady. She has so much in her favour. Her Harry Potter books are credited with rekindling adolescent literacy across the globe. She gives to charity. She's kind to kids. She keeps Highland estate agents in lavish commissions. Joanne is clean. She's spotless.

Well, up to a point. For Rowling is also at the heart of a cult, one as dismaying as anything Lord Voldemort might conceive. She is queen of the forcibly repatriated; poster girl for every soul rendered Scottish by order of the native media. Like a transported slave, her origins were rubbed out and overwritten with her new tribal identity. Yet a less Scottish individual you would struggle to find. Raised in Yate, Gloucestershire, an alumna of the university of Exeter, Rowling was English to the core, a daughter of the shires. She moved to London to work as a researcher at Amnesty International. A spell of personal misfortune saw her seek a fresh start, in Edinburgh. She was almost thirty at the time. There, she

wrote *Harry Potter and the Philosopher's Stone*, the first in what would become the best-selling literary series in history. And there too she was co-opted, lock, stock and whisky barrel, into becoming a true-born Scot, constant focus of beamingly proud Scottish news coverage, inscribed without consultation onto the souvenir tea-towel of Caledonia's glories.

She is not alone. By the day grows the list of forcibly repatriated Scots: rock musicians Mark Knopfler, Rod Stewart and David Byrne; tycoon Donald Trump; authors George Orwell, Joseph Conrad and Dan Brown; even the Biblical baddie Pontius Pilate. One English rock group, The Darkness, are taken to be Scottish because its bass player grew up here. Over the past two decades Scottishness has become like garlic: should you brush against it you will reek of it long afterwards. Possess the slightest genealogical connection to the old country and, *ipso facto*, you're considered Scottish. This scale of tenuousness knows no lower limit. The slimmest familial or biographical pretext will ensure your place in the body of the kirk.

Frequently things get silly. For example, where would you find a garden commemorating the late John Lennon? New York, you answer correctly. But where in Scotland? The village of Durness, on the furthest northern coast. Why? Because Lennon visited the village several times as a child. He made a sentimental return in 1969 and was hospitalised on crashing his car in Golspie. So many happy memories. The whole McLennon deal did seem unusually rum. Generations of genuine Sutherlanders have lived and died and invented useful implements for harvesting mangold-wurzels and the like yet few are remembered with their own memorial garden; while Lennon got one on the strength of a weekend mini-break.

Or consider the publication several years back of a poll naming the greatest Scottish books of all time, a poll that stretched the definition of 'Scottish' books to include Ukrainians writing about the Belgian Congo, Englishmen writing about Eurasia and, most comically of all, the scribes of the Old and New Testaments, few of whom, so far as we know, experienced the sting of summer rain on the Saltcoats seafront.

A variant of the phenomenon pertains to art. For over 200 years, a much-loved painting, 'The Revd Walker Skating on Duddingston Loch' was taken to be the work of Sir Henry Raeburn. That was, until Stephen Lloyd, a curator at the Scottish National Portrait Gallery, realised the painting was of dimensions in which Raeburn seldom painted. Lloyd attributed the work to Henri-Pierre Danloux, a French court artist who escaped to Edinburgh during the revolution. For Danloux to be admitted into the society of semi-Scots would involve admitting an iconic Scottish artwork wasn't as Scottish as thought. Truly a Catch-22.

The 100 Best Scottish Books of All Time were more tenuous still, taking in *Heart of Darkness* by Joseph Conrad, *Nineteen Eighty-Four* by George Orwell and the King James Bible. The usual nationalist apologists popped up to trumpet the usual alibis: that the new Scotland was 'inclusive' and 'open-minded'; useful euphemisms for 'desperate' and 'duplicitous'. Conrad appeared because his novella was published first in the Edinburgh periodical *Blackwood's*. Orwell's novel (or some of it) was written on the island of Jura. It appeared in spite of Orwell's well-reported loathing for all things Scottish; Bernard Crick's biography notes of Orwell's relationship with Scottish acquaintances that he 'crossed the street rather than pass the Muirs, so strong was his irrational dislike of the Scots'.

These weak but ingenious stabs at inclusion are in a long if not noble tradition, stretching back to Bonnie Prince Charlie, a

Hanoverian born in Rome and a commander of the French expeditionary forces, appointed an honorary Scot by the Highland clans in their struggle to depose George II. Similarly, Mary Queen of Scots spent her first two decades in France. But ethnic conscription has come into its own in the modern celebrity age, catalysed by the needs of native media outlets and to prop up the project of nationalism. It is a curious fact that show business in the mid-20th-century was thick with names – Stan Laurel, David Niven, Sandy Mackendrick, Donald Cammell, David McCallum – whose Scottish connections went unremarked in their heydays while, these days, even the most tenuously-connected are lauded as true born sons or daughters of Scotia.

The process really began gathering momentum in the early 1970s with Rod Stewart, London-born but bent on honouring his Glaswegian father by attending Hampden Park with Britt Ekland whenever he could. Stewart is untypical as a co-opted quasi-Scot, however, in that it was his own idea to emphasise his roots. Had he not done so, it may have taken twenty years before some self-appointed mole from the Ministry of Scottishness unearthed the information that would confirm the singer's ethnicity. We live now in an age of photocopy Scots, the links growing fainter with each new edition. The actress Keira Knightley is treated as Scottish because her mother is Scottish, a formulation tried out first with Emma Thompson. The actor Stephen Fry is on the list for serving as rector of a Scottish university, criteria that would merit the inclusion of Winnie Mandela. Donald Trump's determination to build a golf course in Aberdeenshire was attributed not to commercial imperatives but to his mother's origins on the Isle of Lewis. Gordon Ramsay, meanwhile, is the Loch Ness monster of ethnic conscription, his Scottishness confirmed only by a grainy snap of him in a Rangers strip.

At the same time, look at the rogue's gallery of undisputed, fully-certificated Scots: George Galloway, Billy Connolly, Sir Fred Goodwin, Brian Souter, Alex Salmond. Who, then, can blame us for running into the street, grabbing the first foreigner going by and getting all genealogical on them? A more charitable explanation comes from the philosopher Roger Scruton: 'Nations,' he wrote in *England: An Elegy*, 'are, in Benedict Anderson's illuminating phrase, "imagined communities".' And imaginations seldom come more fertile than those of the Scots. As is amply demonstrated by the extravagant fantasias of our very own J.K. Rowling . . .

Alex Salmond

Perhaps you've heard of Godwin's law? It was formulated by American lawyer and internet expert Mike Godwin, to describe a phenomenon spotted frequently on the web. 'As an online discussion grows longer,' Godwin stated, 'the probability of a comparison involving Nazis or Hitler approaches.' In other words, in any heated exchange, on a newsgroup or message board, the patience of participants frays exponentially, resulting finally in one party denouncing their opponent for being as extreme or as deluded as the German demagogue.

Spectacularly, in April, 2012, the law was demonstrated. David Starkey, constitutional historian and dedicated contrarian, took to a conference stage and described Alex Salmond, leader of the Scottish National Party and First Minister of Scotland, as a 'democratic Caledonian Hitler'. In most contexts, the invocation of Godwin's law is considered intellectual bad form, a recourse to the most simplistic and shocking analogy history affords us. The comment was pretty much in character, Starkey being the so-called 'rudest man in Britain'. Starkey has long delighted in saying the unsayable, particularly about the Scots, a race he says he considers to be provincial mediocrities. His Hitler jibe could be dismissed easily, then. Or, just maybe, it couldn't. It is difficult still to banish a suspicion that a considerable number of Scots made a party in

their hearts on hearing his verdict. While Salmond's government is judged to have been competent and constructive, the man himself can set teeth on edge. Scotland almost has a dual leadership; the SNP, those busy, beavering, rebutting worker bees; and, way above them, Salmond, Grand Pooh-bah, the strutting and chortling frontman, his eyes agleam with the lustre of the glittering prize.

Perhaps Starkey got it half-right; Salmond is redolent more of the version of Hitler rendered in Chaplin's 1940 film *The Great Dictator*. There is something faintly comic to the man, with his well-padded girth and slight speech impediment turning *th* into *f*. He is very clearly overweight, a veritable triple-chinned blimp of a bloke, yet he presides over a singularly nannyish, health-touting administration. He is bumptious and incapable of politesse, turning every session of First Minister's Questions into a cawing, boastful display of SNP triumphalism – for who needs politesse when the cause of Scottish independence is so self-evidently just?

Salmond also has, innately, that single quality which sits particularly uneasily with Scots; smugness, for the perceived effectiveness with which the SNP has filled the vacuum left by the implosion of Scottish Labour; for his own mastery of detail and fine print; smugness in his conviction that by the very fact of its existence the SNP has won the moral argument. He has patented, therefore, a particular trademark, the small, pitying chuckle and shake of the head that follows any opponent laying out their case, almost as if he were dealing, more in sorrow than anger, with an idiot or a ranting zealot in the student union. This chuckle, heard every time Salmond was queried by politician or broadcaster, is aggravating in the extreme. It is emblematic of a man so sunken in self-regard he feels sorry for anyone who will not see the light. Altogether, then, Salmond is a most resistible fellow, neither manly nor persuasive, less leader than waddler; arrogant and peevish too, and amused deeply by the reluctance of others to accept his point. He is too wily to express any explicit anti-English sentiment though it is intuited and inferred from so much he says and does, such as his churlish reluctance to welcome the Olympic achievements of Team GB.

When Salmond was leading a minority administration he was merely an irritant, a lesion on the body politic. This changed in 2012 when the nationalists assumed a majority in Holyrood and were in a position to introduce their referendum on the independence question. This particular evolution proved bittersweet. On one hand, we saw and heard more than ever from Salmond. On the other, we had the pleasure of watching his dreams unravel. The countdown to the referendum saw open season declared, as the hard practicalities of independence came home to roost.

Salmond withstood the onslaught poorly, on one issue particularly. Asked on television whether the Scottish government had sought legal advice on the possibility of an independent Scotland joining the European Union, Salmond replied it had. The assertion proved inaccurate, however. The revelation occasioned in Salmond's lieutenants much ingenious back-pedalling, to the effect that though Salmond had answered yes he would have gone on to qualify his answer had he not been interrupted by the interviewer. The debacle soon assumed the pedantic absurdism of Bill Clinton questioning what the definition of *is* is. The lieutenants were not believed and Salmond's credibility was seriously injured.

Not every wound was self-inflicted, however. As the referendum campaign gathered momentum the Conservative government in Westminster, long inclined to regard Scottish nationalism as ointment regards flies, took increasing delight in placing obstacles in the path of its foe. After legal consultation it announced any independent Scotland would be required to renegotiate from scratch its obligations under no less than 8,500 international treaties. Claims made by the Scottish government that the nation would continue in its membership of the United Nations and the IMF were described as 'at best inconclusive'. Cabinet minister Philip Hammond was sent north to describe Salmond's plans for defending Scotland as 'juvenile' and 'woefully thin', opinions many experts queued up to endorse. An independent Scotland, we learned, would be denied a role in setting policy for the Bank of England or the pound even if it were to form a currency union with the UK. Time and again, European officials queried Salmond's assertion that Scotland would be allowed a frictionless entry into the European Union.

So, a Caledonian Hitler? Well, certainly Salmond has strong opinions on ethnic integrity. While the SNP government has been commendably proactive in ensuring that Scotland emphasises its multicultural credentials there's no arguing Salmond's suscepti-bility to even the most hokey manifestations of Caledonian culture. Nothing is excluded, from Kenneth McKellar to shinty, from Burns to PVC kilts. The very fact of Scottishness is sufficient to guarantee virtue. Race is the sole criterion for inclusion in his panoply of glory. This, clearly, is a man who believes that by being born Scottish he has drawn the winning ticket in the lottery of life. The belief is pathological, and not shared by very many Scots, as the opinion polls show consistently, with support for independ-ence having run at thirty per cent for over two decades. He has learnt to temper any scepticism or grudge he may hold towards the English, certainly as long as his ambitions balance on a knife edge. He may yet fulfil those ambitions. If he does, it would be a black day for the nation that this preening, big-talking chump so adores.

Frank Searle

Drumnadrochit is worth a visit, it really is. Nowhere is quite like it. It lies approximately a mile inland of Loch Ness; a douce, decent Highland village, hotspot of shinty and of pony trekking, though it isn't these that give the place its atmosphere. The monster does that; the huge aquatic creature that has legendarily been doing lengths of the twenty-three-mile loch since time immemorial.

The alleged monster's proximity does something unique. It makes Drumnadrochit a weird and lovely locale of whimsy; a kind of Brigadoon with outboard motors. The villagers take half-seriously the possibility that close by lives a reptilian throwback that has survived centuries without any apparent food source, being spotted only by those who haven't quite mastered the zoom or focus functions of their cameras. Visit any other village and ask if anyone has seen The Monster and you'd be kept talking while the butterfly net was fetched. But not here. Each resident has a tale to tell, a yarn to unspool; a party piece, polished over the years to a standard that would shame Peter Ustinov. Is the tale true? Certainly not. Does it matter? Not particularly. The game is the thing. Drumnadrochit lives by weaving a spell, by offering enchantment; an odd Scottish type of enchantment, admittedly, but enchantment nonetheless, brewed from folklore and marine biology, wishful thinking and prehistoric geology. So, those who prize the willing suspension of disbelief are well advised to avoid the theatre (they would be anyway) and head instead, with all haste, to Drumnadrochit.

This is what the late Frank Searle did, in 1969, at the age of forty-eight. Searle had served as an army captain, losing the lower half of his left leg in Palestine, then he worked as a greengrocer in London. Here, fatefully, he came upon a book, *More Than A Legend* by Constance Whyte. Published in 1957, it was a collection of first-hand accounts of the monster, and analysis of the particular geologic properties of Loch Ness. Whyte concluded the loch did indeed contain a creature, a plesiosaur, stranded by landscape change millennia earlier. For his own reasons Searle found the argument persuasive, threw up the life he knew and relocated to Loch Ness, where he established himself in a caravan by the shore. He would become was what he went on to describe in his autobiography as a Monster-Hunter Extraordinary. And hunt is what he did. Each morning, Searle and his binoculars would scan the vast, grey expanse of the loch and register mournfully the sad fact that, yet again, nothing seemed to be doing.

Time passed but Searle's belief in the creature didn't, mainly because he had taken to manufacturing the supporting evidence. From around 1972, with astonishing frequency, his shots of Nessie filled the papers. At the outset, the photographs were indeterminate and rudimentary: monochrome images of undulatory shapes captured from a distance. Seen today, the images couldn't be less convincing if they featured Nessie posing with a beach ball. But these were simpler times. As if to emphasise the fact, Searle took to assembling his images using dinosaur postcards purchased in local shops. It mattered naught. Newspaper sales figures, and thereby the commercial viability of Searle's pictures, reflected no distinction between faked Nessie pictures and flagrantly faked Nessie pictures. Searle's small cupful measure of renown scarcely diminished. Nessie-hunting became a craze and Searle was its ringmaster, sporting a badge stating 'I'm Nearly Famous' and attempting to fill his caravan with a harem of 'monster huntresses' – young female admirers willing to share with Searle watching duties, at the very least. New recruits were found through ads in newspapers that served areas with high unemployment.

The set-up was, for a while, in its way, really quite agreeable, for Searle certainly: a simple, sedentary sex-filled life subsidised by the very same credulous newspapers who created and spread Searle's spurious fame. Of course it couldn't last, and it didn't. Searle was undone by a pincer movement. On one flank was American explorer Robert Rines, who in the mid-1970s investigated the loch with sonar equipment, just as the Loch Ness and Morar Project (LNMP) began undertaking biological surveys. Rines particularly redefined the field, capturing a set of underwater images that felt infinitely more plausible than Searle's school-project prefabrications. Searle didn't give up without a fight, though; quite literally. He attached a note reading 'Your time is running out' to the window of a car owned by one Tony Harmsworth, founder of the Official Loch Monster Exhibition in Drumnadrochit. He launched a Molotov cocktail at a boat belonging to the LNMP. Locals turned against him. He attempted one last hurrah, with photographs depicting a flying saucer hovering over the loch. It came too late. The moment had passed. Searle's return felt like that of a jaded pop star, chancing his arm one last time before capitulating to a life driving cabs. He departed the Highlands in the early 1980s, dying in Fleetwood, Lancashire in 2005.

By most accounts Searle was an unpleasant man. Adrian Shine, a veteran of Loch Ness scientific study, described him as a 'hard-bitten, suspicious, shifty character, a chap with chips on both shoulders'. Normally, these would be meagre grounds on which to argue the man had exerted adverse effect upon Scotland. All manner of public figures are suspicious and shifty; why single out Searle?

Well, because of the *what* and the *when*. The *why* takes care of itself. As with all snake-oil salesmen, Searle's needs were simple: a bit of cash, a television camera to talk into, comely young women whose blouses wouldn't stay buttoned. In this regard, Searle was standard-issue: a blackguard and footpad; a conman with a holdall full of four-pound notes. Searle's moral sense, evidently, was as murky as the bottom of the loch itself. His timing wasn't much better. Accounts of the monster went back as far as the first century yet Searle set up operations just as science was striving, finally, to get the mystery addressed. Searle became the clown in the laboratory. He turned something with a strange and plangent significance – the vast, unknowable loch and its legends – into low comedy. For the monster has long been in delicate suspension. The Scots are not like the Irish, with their leprechauns and their Blarney stone. They know fine well that the Loch Ness monster does not exist. But they know also that mystery, awe and terror do, as symbolised by that silly immortal dinosaur. Scotland had already placed that particular tongue in its cheek; it hardly needed a hand from Frank Searle.

Tommy Sheridan

Nothing in the annals of political outlandishness prepares the unwitting for the saga of Tommy Sheridan. Nothing. *Nothing.* In the wake of Sheridan, an observer might be told the Prime Minister was *in flagrante* with members of the Basil Brush Appreciation Society and wouldn't turn a hair. If invited to watch a leading Anglican Archbishop be painted in oils while performing gender reassignment upon Sir Bruce Forsyth, a Sheridan veteran would yawn and scrutinise her fingernails. This was the Sheridan effect. It made perverts and fetishists of all who encountered it.

In the 1990s and noughties Sheridan was a politician, a relatively big wheel in the gerbil cage that is Holyrood. His beliefs were of a markedly radical stripe. He came from Pollok in the south of the city, an interzone of estates and graffitied fridges in front gardens; a stronghold of real Glaswegians being frightfully plain-spoken, usually on the subject of how they came by the injuries to their faces. Sheridan founded and headed the Scottish Socialist Party, a combustible crew of fist-clenchers and placard-wavers. Much to his delight, he was jailed several times, having opposed more stridently than the law permitted whatever happened to be getting his goat that week. There was a time when Sheridan was hauled off to the cells regularly, often in the company of fellow hard leftist

George Galloway, for breaching the peace around various nuclear naval facilities.

No gathering was too small for Sheridan to dust down his megaphone and dispense whatever Utopian eyewash he thought would gratify his unskilled, low-income constituency on the living curling fringes of sink-estate Scotland: Scottish independence, free school meals, increased taxes for the wealthy, the legalisation of cannabis, renaming Glasgow's airport William Wallace International. In his personal life, meanwhile, he was, famously, a teetotal, non-smoking amateur footballer, and devoted husband to the comically fearsome Gail, a trolley dolly with British Airways. He was a man who in every sense of the phrase embodied the principles, not to mention the physiognomy, of muscular socialism.

Sheridan nursed also a deep attachment to sunbed culture. He made no secret of his twice-weekly visits to tanning parlours. Over the years they turned him an unsettling shade of Tango-marinaded mahogany. In hindsight, this predilection for auto-immolation should have been the giveaway. It suggested a sensual side to the man, a concern with, if not the pleasures of the flesh, then certainly the hue and texture of it. Such did not occur, however. He was a textbook revolutionary Marxist living in suburban bliss with a no-nonsense wife whose tongue could break a swan's wing at fifty paces. His cover was good.

It was blown, so to speak, on 31 October 2004, when the Scottish edition of the *News of the World* carried a front-page splash: Married MSP is Spanking Swinger. Recounting a visit made by a group of friends to a sex club in Manchester named Cupid's, the story didn't identify Sheridan but the picture it drew was of a genteel depravity unglimpsed since the days of Cynthia Payne, with casual liaisons in darkened rooms, habitués playing snooker wearing nipple clamps and a politician who ached to be spanked by women wearing red PVC gloves. Rumours of the MSP's identity raged through Holyrood's parliamentary corridors. Ten days later, Sheridan called a press conference in the parliament's canteen to announce his resignation as convener of the SSP, ostensibly to devote himself to Gail as she underwent the latter stages of a difficult pregnancy. The following Sunday, the *News of the World* delivered the *coup de grâce*: My Kinky Four-in-a-Bed Orgy with Tommy, the recollections of a former escort girl and SSP worker who claimed she and Sheridan began to meet for sex months after the MSP had married his childhood sweetheart Gail: 'He wanted me to do a lot of stuff to him, smacking and talking dirty, tying him up,' revealed the Deep Throat. 'He liked rough stuff. He likes uniforms.' Asked, in a way perhaps that revealed more about the interrogator than the subject, if Sheridan enjoyed being whipped, she replied: 'Just a little bit. Nothing too harsh. At the top of his legs.' Sheridan immediately set about suing the newspaper.

When the defamation case finally reached the Sheriff Court in Edinburgh, the initial allegations had been augmented by further dirt. A woman named Ann Colvin claimed she'd attended a stag party in Glasgow's Moat House hotel in 2002 at which she saw Sheridan indulge in group sex with a prostitute and a well-known footballer; Sheridan's father-in-law supplied him with an alibi. Gail Sheridan chipped in with paperwork she said proved her husband could not have been there. Meanwhile, the *News of the World* columnist claimed their trip to Manchester had been preceded by an afternoon threesome in a Glasgow flat during which Sheridan was joined by his brother-in-law, Andy McFarlane. Technically, of course, this didn't constitute incest, though most men would be happy to let the finer points of the debate slide. Sheridan's aged mother Alice attended each day of the trial. It is every man's Freudian nightmare to have his sexual behaviour mentioned within a mile of his mother. The defence should have known this and capitalised upon it, dispensing with cross-examination to tell the judge: 'My lord, this is a newspaper headline concerning the plaintiff's alleged fetish for sex involving stilettos and ice cubes. And this is my client's mother. We rest our case.'

As it was, they did not. And, anyway, in a sensational move, Sheridan would fire his counsel on the trial's ninth day and represent himself, provoking much newspaper hilarity about Tommy dropping his briefs. Of these new responsibilities he made heavy work, revealing he could not operate his court-provided laptop and receiving from Lord Turnbull impromptu instruction in Windows XP: 'If you press Search, then Document search,' instructed the judge from the bench, 'then type in the word you're looking for, that should take you to it.' Nearly half of the public gallery was occupied by older women in primary-coloured leisure-wear, their beefy upper arms untroubled by anything so formal as a sleeve. Some were accompanied by bags of supermarket shopping that rustled as they shifted their feet. During each break in proceedings they produced packets of Regal cigarettes and bustled eagerly for the exits. They were Sheridan's family and friends and they lent a gamey, militantly partisan tone to proceedings. At one point they were admonished by the judge for 'audible scoffing'.

Amazingly, Sheridan won the case. Two factors were thought influential: the tough-but-tender testimony of Gail Sheridan and the fact that Marxists, particularly *en masse,* could squabble bewilderingly with a black cat in a darkened room. Few imagined Sheridan would get away with it: rumours about him had been flying round the city for years. Somehow, though, he did, and won £200,000 in damages. His victory celebrations were as jubilant as the *News of the World* was bemused: 'What we have done in the last five weeks,' Sheridan shouted at cameras, 'is the equivalent of

Gretna taking on Real Madrid in the Bernabéu and beating them on penalties.'

Some while later, however, it occurred to police that, with so much testimony against him, Sheridan may have fibbed under oath. In 2007 he was charged with perjury. In 2010 a trial followed, this time in Glasgow, this time with Sheridan on the defensive. More of the same followed: more pointy recriminations as to who spanked who and where they bought the equipment. Again, Sheridan dismissed his counsel and performed the job himself. Again, former comrades set to clawing one another's eyes out. All that differed was the outcome: Sheridan was convicted of perjury and sentenced to three years imprisonment. Repetition and over-familiarity, it seemed, had rather soured the presumption that Sheridan, the one-time poster boy of civil disobedience, could have found himself so unjustly compromised by mere circumstance. He spent a year in Barlinnie and, still protesting his innocence, is now co-convenor of Solidarity, another Trotskyist gaggle. From a position where once it held six seats in the Scottish parliament, the SSP was in ruins, as was the reputation of the hard left in Scotland. Making the Sheridan affair the definitive case of easy come, easy go.

Jack Vettriano

' I don't know much about art but I know what I like'-- we hear this phrase frequently. It alludes to a division that has vexed us since Duchamp exhibited his first urinal, namely that art exists in two distinct forms, for two opposed purposes. On one hand, it operates for its own sake, *ars gratia aria*, as an ongoing investigation into visual expression, into what we look at and what it tells us. When audiences witnessed, for instance, Richard Hamilton's 1956 photomontage *Just What Is It That Makes Today's Home So Different, So Appealing?*, with its cut-out snaps of bodybuilders and movie starlets relaxing in a suburban living room, they were bemused. Surely, they harrumphed, rubbish like *this* can't be art? But the shock passed and now we see Hamilton's work for what it was, a prophesy of the media age with its threatened glut of beguiling tinsel.

Warhol, Lichtenstein, Koons and Peter Blake had similar insights. So much art once seemed weird and impenetrable, and then the penny dropped. Presumably it will do so one day with the head-scratching works of Hirst and Emin, even with those piles of bricks in the Tate. But art has a second purpose, of a more practical kind; to be hung on the walls of homes, pubs and restaurants, to gratify the eye by being just what it appears to be, whether that is a bowl of fruit or a gang of cheerful bulldogs playing poker. This is art as decoration and those invested in the former frown upon it terribly.

And quite correctly. Prints and posters are mass-produced media and the public's stated taste is for the pretty, the silly and the sentimental. Decorative art of this sort is, by definition, ghastly, utterly non-PLU, chosen only to complement a colour scheme or to suggest a resident's interests. Think, for instance, of the nightmarish daubs of Beryl Cook, with their lardy ladies on nights out, as resonant as a cartoon in the *People's Friend*. Try recalling when last you sat in a restaurant whose walls were not hung with fuzzy monochrome photographs of Manhattan by night. Or think back to the 1970s when every living room displayed the same oval-eyed, raven-haired honey with a come-hither stare, as produced by the Russian artist Vladimir Tretchikoff.

Jack Vettriano, the self-taught former miner from Fife turned millionaire peddler of tasteful erotica, is the Tretchikoff of the modern day. Courtesy of prints, posters and postcards – he is the most reproduced artist presently at work – Vettriano's images are every bit as ubiquitous. Rare is the suburban trattoria or dentist's waiting room without its fading Vettriano print. What the art of Vettriano evokes is redolent of Tretchikoff too: a sultry sense of erotic mystique, embodied in exotic and untouchable sirens. Tretchikoff, though, could have been in little doubt that he was a mere hack; his nickname was the King of Kitsch.

Vettriano himself is not so sanguine. His career has been one long fistfight, as he demands from the art establishment due recognition and the art establishment maintains, regretfully, that Vettriano couldn't be trusted to paint a garden shed. In his own mind, Vettriano, defiantly maintaining his shabbily stubbled chic into his seventh decade, is a proper artist, pouring his soul onto canvas as Picasso and Bacon did before him. In those minds that matter, meanwhile, he is a ham-fisted amateur, and a rather dubious one at that, clearly in the grip of an overmastering sexual compulsion, echoed in the soft-porn sheen of his work. 'He can't paint, he just colours in,' was the opinion of Sandy Moffat of the Glasgow School of Art; 'I'd be more than happy to say that we think him an indifferent painter and that he is very low down our list of priorities,' said Richard Calvacoressi, former director of the Scottish National Gallery of Modern Art.

The face-off has been ongoing since Vettriano came to prominence in the early 1990s. It is the perfect encapsulation of the core debate on art and its appreciation. Many thousands adore his work, find it mysterious and sexy, with its *femme fatales* and 1940s gumshoes transacting midnight trysts, rendered in tones as deep and luxurious as old movie posters. Some of his paintings are, as people these days will insist on putting it, iconic: his most famed work, 'The Singing Butler', sold at auction in 2004 for £744, 000. Aha, the Vettriano apologist will crow, proof of the fellow's artistic merit. The price tag was proof of no such thing, of course, so much as proof that art speculation thrives. Such profiteers took a bath in 2010 when seven of ten Vettrianos offered at Sotheby's failed to sell while the three that did sell went for half their previous prices.

Two years prior to its sale *The Singing Butler* had been rejected for the Royal Academy summer exhibition. Neither will you find Vettriano in the National Gallery, Tate Modern or Tate Britain. As one, the citadels turned their backs to him. Only two of his paintings are on public display, both in Kirkcaldy, both donated by the artist himself. All quite understandable, particularly since news that a number of characters in his paintings, including 'The Singing Butler', had been lifted directly from *The Illustrator's Figure Reference Manual*, a technical guide published in 1987. Vettriano's get-out was weaselly in the extreme, with its claim that

Francis Bacon owned a copy of the same book: 'If it's good enough for Bacon,' he countered, offering no evidence that Bacon ever copied anything, 'it's good enough for me. I was accused of plagiarism. Bloody bastards.' When the controversy blew over, Vettriano contacted the model he'd transplanted from the manual to 'The Singing Butler': 'I thought it would be lovely to paint her again,' he said, rather overstating the extent to which he'd painted her previously. 'She didn't want to do it.'

And who could blame her? What woman but the most damaged exhibitionist could bear it, to be confined in a garret as Vettriano watches you tighten your suspender belt and slip into your stilettos, his wily old eyes lingering upon every adjustment to every strap? The thought is too ghastly for words. The objectification of women in Vettriano's work is obvious and oft-remarked (its objectification of butlers is rarely mentioned), all to a degree that shuts down the debate, renders it too tired to be mentioned. Vettriano's work normalises the predatory gaze, particularly so given its ubiquity. This cannot be a good thing.

But, then, so little connected with Vettriano is a good thing: his petulance when experts can't help but notice his want of competence, his belief that all criticism is merely envy, his queasy fetishism, his mechanical, made-to-order, by-the-yard creative method, his insistence that earnings are index-linked to talent. But, most of all, the extent to which Scotland seems proud of this pervy charlatan. In 2010, the MSP Ted Brocklebank, seldom a man to flinch from seeing his name in the paper, filed a motion in Parliament calling for official recognition of Vettriano's contribution to Scottish culture. The howling, philistinic populism of this boils the blood. Perhaps the politician was wearing a basque beneath his suit.

And Never Brought To Mind . . .

The following individuals have done their own bits to ruin Scotland, and will no doubt do more given the chance.

Joel Barnett – When Chief Secretary to the Treasury in the 1970s, Barnett drew up an equation to determine levels of public expenditure. The Barnett Formula became famed for its impenetrability, more so when yoked to its Scottish cousin, the West Lothian Question. Both led to ongoing uncertainty as to whether England subsidised Scotland or vice versa. Even yet, when the formula is mentioned, economists fake hiccups.

John Barrowman – The very definition of the performer who does twenty minutes when the fridge light comes on, Barrowman is a pathological kind of character, forcefully insistent we appreciate the breadth and depth, not to mention the width, of his facility for the arts of variety. You name it and Barrowman will attempt it, teeth shining like a lighthouse lamp, tendons itching to form a pair of jazz hands. What a ghastly, grinning cut-price sub-Broadway chump he is.

David Coulthard – Formula One drivers are seldom likeable, if only because they get to spray champagne over Brazilian lingerie models while three men in a fork-lift truck transport their wages to the desired spot. Yet even by the standards of his trade, Coulthard seems something of a twerp: irritable, graceless and flash. All the envious onlooker could have over Coulthard is their non-possession of such a preposterous, rectilinear jaw.

Alan Hansen – Formerly the suave, oily dispenser of Colemanballs on Saturday night football round-ups, Hansen clearly sees himself as the Sean Connery of the subs bench, a fine figure of a man with the poise of a born ladykiller. The effect is compromised rather by the fact that he is discussing Tranmere Rovers.

Peter Howson – Scotland loves nothing so much as a lurid depiction of its own debasement. Generally these are delivered by film and television. The fine art side is handled by Howson. His art, technically impressive yet horribly ugly, tends to depict a bizarre sect of muscular, pin-headed proles who model grimy vests while grimacing. Predictably, his work is adored by American celebrities. The rest of us hear his name and let our heads drop to our chests.

Sir Alec Douglas-Home – He is the Conservative leader time forgot, a son of privilege so grand that when his predecessor Macmillan stood down Douglas-Home had to endure the bothersome rigmarole of becoming an MP before he could become Prime Minister. He needn't have bothered. In his year in office, Douglas-Home would have made more noise if he'd positioned himself outside parliament and sold newspapers. He was a prime minister who rose without trace, and sank just as secretly.

The Krankies – Inconceivably sinister husband and wife – yet father and son – entertainment pairing who brought the spirit of 1890s variety theatre to childrens' television. Perhaps suspecting their set-up could be creepier still the pair went on, quite voluntarily, to disclose their passion for swinging and wife-swapping. Society felt something walk over its grave.

Annie Lennox – Once an impressively mellifluous vocalist and songwriter, Lennox tumbled late in her career into the swamp of celebrity mercy deliverance, forever wearing her sad face to visit refugee camps with Bono and Lenny Henry. As with all members of the concerned showbiz wealthy, we wondered what prevented her writing a cheque for five million then shutting up. Insufficiently conspicuous, we suppose.

Andrew Neil – Self-styled international playboy publisher, former editor of the *Sunday Times* and television interpreter for the centre-right, Neil is shackled forever by the insistence of *Private Eye* on running in every issue a snap of him in sports vest and baseball cap, squiring an unidentified dusky companion. Quite why the magazine insists upon this malicious, juvenile, repetitive, delightful and utterly hilarious jape we couldn't say . . .

Gillian McKeith – Now by-passed rather, McKeith and her nutritional finger-wagging were everywhere for a spell. She nursed a particular, and somewhat nauseating, fascination for the yuckier aspects of the digestive journey, examining stool samples and the like. Undone somewhat by several controversies relating to her academic credentials. Like a goju berry flapjack, she is bound to return.

Michelle Mone – While unqualified to discuss the comfort afforded by the push-up bras she manufactures, we do note ruefully that Mone has spent two decades as a living soap opera, squabbling with celebrities, transacting divorces and queening it over the smutty, innuendo-laden world you'd expect was inhabited by those involved with lingerie in west-central Scotland.

Neil Oliver – Glossily-tressed television historian given to striding over mountainsides in helicopter shot while discoursing upon Scotland's lot, truly a woeful tale his programmes do their utmost to prolong. Quickly, Oliver's polytechnic lecturer tones rivalled the Go Compare commercial as an urgent inducement to change channel.

Ian Rankin – The novelist of choice for those embarking on long train journeys without having brought something to read, Rankin has kept railway station newsagents in business with his inexplicably popular crime fictions. Queasily imitative of proper writing, his books bring into the modern day the mysteries of old Edinburgh. Among these mysteries, Rankin's appeal must now be considered foremost.

Iain Duncan Smith – A classic example of the Scottish tendency to select who is and isn't native, Duncan Smith was raised in Edinburgh, though we hear little of the fact. Quite understandable given the controversy around his welfare reforms and the low comedy he engendered as Conservative leader with his The Quiet Man is Here to Stay speech.

Sir Basil Spence – The name of Spence, though applauded elsewhere, particularly for his resurrection of the bombed Coventry Cathedral, is excoriated in Glasgow still. The Edinburgh architect designed the infamous Hutchesontown C flats in the Gorbals, which were loathed almost immediately upon completion in 1962 for their susceptibility to damp and for their vogueish boxiness. While it is always encouraging to hear a Glaswegian express a view on architecture, local opinion of Spence, even since the blocks were demolished, remains as brutal as his architecture.

Andy Stewart – The kilted entertainer remains the voodoo dolly of Scotland, a personification of all that was feared; a purveyor of twinkly, twee kitsch concerning the domestic movements of wee mice and suchlike. The merest sight of his brogues, Argyle socks and jigging pins brings it all back, but with no attendant irony, nostalgia or sentiment.

Nicola Sturgeon – Deputy First Minister in the SNP executive, Sturgeon fancies she is the nation's headmistress, even if she is faintly comic with her air of tested patience and her rigid, breakable hair. When she discusses fiscal policy one feels a Pavlovian urge to finish one's homework and have a bath before bedtime, so convincing is Sturgeon's approximation of an exasperated supply teacher. Barely in her forties, she appears to dress by raiding the wardrobe of a late aunt.

The Tartan Army – Insanity, said Einstein, was doing the same thing repeatedly while expecting a different outcome. Presumably his theory of relativity allowed Einstein to zip forward in time and look upon the Tartan Army, given name of the gaggle of twerps who turn out whenever the Scottish national football team takes the field. Time and again they travel to some godless region of Latvia, dressed as walking adverts for porridge oats; time and again they see the Scots humbled by a team of Slavic postmen. Of course, the entire charade is really just a pretext for heavy drinking and wife avoidance.

David Tennant – Irritatingly pretty and shamelessly ubiquitous actor, with only two modes; hysteria and glumness. The former was useful during his tenure as *Doctor Who*, which he spent running down corridors, explaining gadgets at the top of his voice. He is glum in everything else, as if he'd received a tax bill moments before the cameras rolled. Every male thirtysomething actor in the land will be sticking pins in his effigy.

Midge Ure – Hopeless pop gadfly whose commendation to posterity is that Bob Geldof did him up like a kipper at Live Aid. Prior to this, Ure had a nation biting its lower lip to stifle mirth while he swanned around with New Romantic brickies Ultravox. A dilettante who made a little go a long way, Ure is remembered best for the refrain to his biggest hit, 'Vienna': 'This means nothing to me!' he howled. A nation knew the feeling.

Kirsty Young – Not since the days of Margaret Thatcher have we seen, or more correctly heard, an example of voice coaching so noticeable as the one offered by Kirsty Young. When she presented on Scottish Television she was standard-issue well-spoken. Now, on *Desert Island Discs* and *Crimewatch*, she resembles a beauty therapist doing her impression of Orson Welles. Very curious.